The National Health
Program Book

The National Health Program Book

A Source Guide for Advocates

David U. Himmelstein, M.D.
&
Steffie Woolhandler, M.D., M.P.H.

Common Courage Press   Monroe, Maine

**Library of Congress
Cataloging-in-Publication-Data**

Himmelstein, David U.
The National Health Program book :
a source guide for advocates /
David U. Himmelstein & Steffie Woolhandler.
p. cm.
Includes bibliographical references.
ISBN 1-56751-019-1. -- ISBN 1-56751-018-3 (pbk.)
1. Medicine, State--Canada. 2. Medicine, State--United States. 3. Medical policy--Canada. 4. Medical policy--United States. 5. Insurance, health--Canada. 6. Insurance, health--United States.
I. Woolhandler, Steffie.   II. Title.
RA412.5.C3H56   1994
362. 1'0973--dc20   93-21047
CIP

Common Courage Press
Box 702
Monroe, ME 04951
207-525-0900 fax: 207-525-3068

First Printing

Contents

Part I
The Economic Context of the Health Care Crisis: Rising Costs, Declining Coverage and Incomes

Part II
The Impact of the Crisis:
Care Denied and Delayed

Part III
The Social Cost of the American System:
Poor Health Care Leads to Poor Health

Part IV
Rationing in the Midst of Plenty

Part V
Exploring the Alternative:
Canada's National Health Program

Part VI
Why Our System Costs More and Delivers Less: Administrative Waste in U.S. Health Care

Part VII
A National Health Program for the U.S.

Part VIII
Paying for a National Health Program

Part IX
President Clinton's Plan:
Making Insurance Companies The Feudal Lords
Of American Medicine

Part X
A Force For Change:
Public Opinion on Health Care Reform

Part XI
A National Health Program for the United States:
A Physicians' Proposal

Introduction:
Ten Myths
About Health Care

There is much confusion over the wisdom of adopting a Canadian-style health care system for the United States. This book argues for such a system and refutes many myths raised by its opponents, including:

Myth 1: *Canadians face long line ups for care.*

Fact: 95 percent of Canadians get the care they need within 24 hours—at least as fast as most Americans. In the past, some Canadians waited for such things as non-emergency coronary artery bypass graft surgery but such waits have decreased in the 1990s. For some kinds of medical conditions, notably breast cancer, Canadians can expect faster treatment than Americans.

Myth 2: *High-tech operations aren't as available in Canada as in the United States.*

Fact: The rate for complicated operations such as heart, kidney, liver, and bone marrow transplants is similar for the two countries. In the United States, operations like coronary bypass are more readily available to those with higher incomes. In Canada, there is no such restriction, and the rate of operations is remarkably even across the income spectrum.

Myth 3: *The health of Canadians is due to factors not related to their health system.*

Fact: Canadian infant mortality, to take one measure of health, was similar to that in the United States prior to implementation of its national health program. Today, it ranks in the top ten countries with the lowest infant mortality rates, while the United States ranks worse than 20th.

Providing quality care to everyone as soon as they need it is a key factor behind Canadians' longer life expectancy— nearly two years longer than Americans'. Canada's drug abuse problems are greater than ours, and healthier "lifestyles" cannot account for Canadians' better health.

Myth 4: *Canadians aren't free to choose their own doctors.*

Fact: Canadians have far greater freedom to choose— virtually unrestricted—than Americans. Many Americans are forced to choose from a limited pool of doctors employed by their health maintenance organizations.

Myth 5: *Changing systems would stifle technological and other types of innovation encouraged by the free market.*

Fact: In 1990, to take a typical year, research output, as measured by the number of medical articles published per capita was about the same in Canada as it was in the United States. Many high-tech innovations—such as bone-marrow transplants—have been developed in Canada.

Myth 6: *Canada's health system costs too much money, and costs are spiraling out of control.*

Fact: Canada's costs are rising much more slowly than U.S. costs, and we now spend $1,000 more per person on health care each year. Further, while Canada spends only 9 percent of its gross national product on health care and insures everyone, we spend 14 percent and leave 37 million uninsured. Competition in the U.S. system has increased costs.

Myth 7: *The Canadian health program is inefficient and costly.*

Fact: Because Canada has a single-payer system instead of several hundred insurance companies that pay for care, administration costs much less than in the United States. For example, in 1993, we paid $911 per person in administrative costs for health care. Canadians paid only $270 per person. Blue Cross of Massachusetts covers 2.7 million subscribers and employs 6,680 people, more than are employed in all of Canada's health care program which ensures 26 million Canadians.

Myth 8: *Such a program would never work here because Americans wouldn't tolerate government interference with the "free market" health care system.*

Fact: Nearly 75% of Americans want a national health insurance system. In a democracy, this should be the number one contender of all health care proposals.

Myth 9: *Doctors are against a national health insurance program and are a key reason why we can't have national health insurance.*

Fact: Most doctors favor some form of national health insurance, though 74% mistakenly believe that most of their colleagues oppose such a measure.

Myth 10: *The Clinton health proposal will solve most of the problems of our health care system.*

Fact: The Clinton administration hopes to save money by pushing most Americans into health maintenance organizations (HMOs), but HMO premiums have been skyrocketing. Furthermore, HMOs and other health plans under managed competition will be rigidly class-stratified, insuring better care for the wealthy. Managed care, the system used by HMOs, works worst for those who are poor and in ill health.

Clinton's Proposal means:
- a few giant insurers/HMOs enroll almost all patients;
- patients are forced into a stripped-down plan chosen by their employer or health insurance purchasing cooperative;
- almost all doctors will be employed by insurers/HMOs;
- almost all hospitals will be controlled by insurers/HMOs;
- multi-tiered care will leave those with less income in poorer health;
- costs will not be contained.

One final myth worth confronting: We can't succeed in getting a national health program that provides universal access to affordable, top-quality care.

<u>Fact:</u> The overwhelming majority of Americans support a national health program modeled on Canada's. Those favoring managed competition are narrow special interests lobbying to keep our inefficient, expensive, and rationed health care system alive.

Since knowledge is power, we offer this book as a tool to cut through the sense of confusion and hopelessness that we can't win against the insurance lobby. We hope readers will use the information to transform the existing consensus into action, applying political pressure on the media to tell it like it is, and on politicians who realize that a dissatisfied electorate is a threat to their jobs.

17

Part I

The Economic Context of the Health Care Crisis: Rising Costs, Declining Coverage and Incomes

This section's charts document a crisis: health costs are skyrocketing while most people's income is stagnating or declining. As a result, more are forced to avoid care they can't afford—often leading to preventable death and disability. Employers, faced with rising costs, are demanding that employees pay a bigger share, financially squeezing many Americans.

Meanwhile, poverty has been on the rise, real wages have declined over the past decade, and the wealthiest ten percent of Americans are amassing phenomenal wealth. U.S. wage earners are poorly compensated in comparison with top management and enjoy less vacation than their counterparts in other countries. Our corporate CEOs reap salaries far above those of their counterparts in Canada, Japan and Germany.

Health Costs Rise 10% in One Year!

RISING HEALTH CARE COSTS

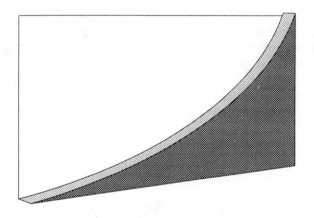

This unlabelled chart depicts the rise of U.S health costs.

Health care costs topped $900 billion in 1993, 14.4% of the Gross National Product (GNP). This is an increase of 10% from 1992, when health care consumed 13.1% of GNP. Health spending has doubled since 1985, when health care accounted for 10.5% of GNP. The Health Care Financing Administration (HCFA) projects that health costs will continue to grow 9.2% per year until the year 2000, unless a major reform is enacted. By the year 2000, health spending will amount to $1.74 trillion, 18.1% of GNP.

Health care cost increases have not slowed despite 20

years of policy explicitly aimed at containing costs and increasing competition. The growth of HMO's, the implementation of the Medicare DRG program, the rapid increase in utilization review and a variety of other bureaucratic measures have had little impact on overall health care costs.

The U.S. spends far more on health care than any other nation, 40% more per person than Canada whose health spending is the second highest. Moreover, the gap between the U.S. and the rest of the world is widening. Most other developed nations have stabilized their health spending at about 8% or 9% of GNP, while our spending continues to soar.

Wages Devoted to Meeting Health Costs on the Rise

WEEKS OF WORK AT AVERAGE WAGE NEEDED TO MEET HEALTH COSTS

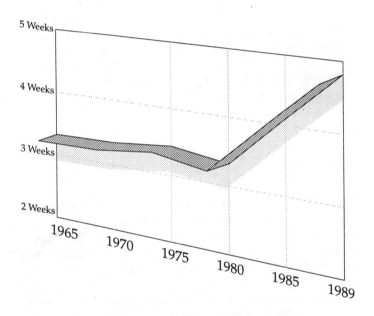

SOURCE: CONGRESSIONAL DEMOCRATIC STUDY GROUP, 1991

Over the past decade, health costs have increased dramatically faster than wages. The rising portion of employee compensation devoted to health care costs constrains the expansion of wages, pensions and other benefits.

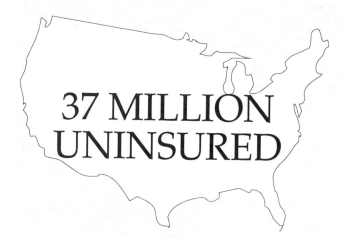

A Country at Risk

37 MILLION UNINSURED

More than 37 million Americans were uninsured during an average month in 1992, according to the Census Bureau's Current Population Survey. This represented 14.7% of the population and was an increase of 2 million from the previous year. Over the past decade the number of uninsured increased by 12 million, and more people are uninsured today than at any time since the passage of Medicare and Medicaid.

In 1991, New England had the lowest rate of uninsurance, 10% of any region, while the West South Central region (Arkansas, Louisiana, Oklahoma and Texas) had the highest rate, 20.8% uninsured. The range for individual states was a low of 7% in Hawaii to a high of 25.7% in the District of Columbia. Hawaii, despite its employer mandate legislation, had an uninsurance rate only slightly lower than Connecticut (7.5%), North Dakota (7.6%) and several other states.

Men are more frequently uninsured than women; 15.8% vs. 12.5%. The poor have the highest rates of uninsurance: 22.6% for those with family incomes below $25,000; 10.2% for those with family incomes between $25,000 and $50,000; and 6.9% for those with family incomes above $50,000 annually. Young adults are the age group most likely to be uninsured: 12.7% of children less than 18 years of age are uninsured; 20.9% of those aged 18 through 39; 12.6% of those aged 40 through 64; and 0.9% of people over the age of 64.

The Number of Uninsured
Rose by Over 50% in 15 years

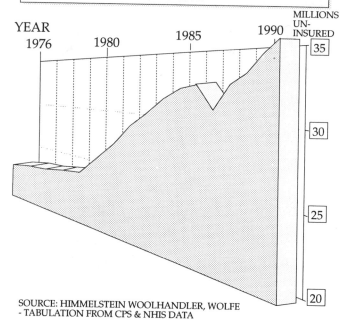

NUMBERS OF UNINSURED AMERICANS
1976-1992

YEAR

1976 1980 1985 1990

MILLIONS UN-INSURED

35

30

25

20

SOURCE: HIMMELSTEIN WOOLHANDLER, WOLFE
- TABULATION FROM CPS & NHIS DATA

In 1991 more people were uninsured than at any time since the passage of Medicare and Medicaid in the mid-1960's. The number of uninsured increased 4 million between 1989 and 1992 following a rise of 700,000 between 1988 and 1989. Overall, about 13 million more people are uninsured today than in 1980.

25% Uninsured at Some Point During a 28 Month Period

NUMBER OF UNINSURED
DURING A 28 MONTH PERIOD, U.S. 1986-1988

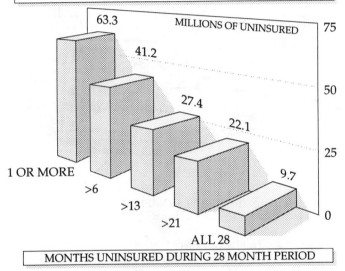

MILLIONS OF UNINSURED

63.3 — 1 OR MORE
41.2 — >6
27.4 — >13
22.1 — >21
9.7 — ALL 28

MONTHS UNINSURED DURING 28 MONTH PERIOD

SOURCE: CURRENT POP. REPTS. P-70, #17

While about 37 million Americans are uninsured at any one time, substantially greater numbers are uninsured for at least some part of the year. During a 28 month period studied by the Census Bureau between 1986 and 1988, 63.3 million were uninsured for at least one month, while 9.7 million were uninsured for the entire period. Thus, about 1/4 of all Americans suffered a spell of uninsurance during a 2 1/3 year period.

Most Uninsured Adults have Jobs

WHO ARE THE UNINSURED?

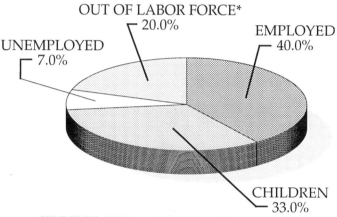

OUT OF LABOR FORCE*
20.0%

UNEMPLOYED
7.0%

EMPLOYED
40.0%

CHILDREN
33.0%

* STUDENTS OVER 18, HOMEMAKERS,
DISABLED, EARLY RETIREES

SOURCE: CENSUS BUREAU, CPS

About two-thirds of the uninsured are employed workers and their families. 13% of full-time workers were uninsured in 1990, while about one-third of the unemployed were without insurance.

Workers in the following industries had uninsurance rates greater than 30%: agriculture, household employment, construction, and forestry and fishing. Those employed in entertainment, retail trade, repair, and personal services (other than household) had uninsurance rates between 20 and 30% in 1990. Only 7% of the uninsured are unemployed adults.

Those Lacking Insurance Come From All Walks of Life

WHO'S UNINSURED?

- 22% OF FAMILIES WITH INCOMES UNDER $25,000
- 8% OF FAMILIES WITH INCOMES OVER $50,000
- 13% OF FULL TIME WORKERS, 1/3 OF THE UNEMPLOYED
- OVER 30% OF WORKERS IN AGRICULTURE, CONSTRUC-
    TION, FORESTRY, FISHING, AND HOUSEKEEPING
- 6% OF MDs, TEACHERS, PROFESSORS
- 16% OF CLERGY
- 33% OF HISPANICS
- NO LEGISLATORS OR JUDGES

SOURCE: HIMMELSTEIN, WOOLHANDLER & WOLFE, 1991 - TABULATIONS FROM CPS

While the poor and minority group members are at highest risk of being uninsured, substantial numbers of people from virtually all walks of life lack coverage. Nearly 33% of Hispanics, 20% of African-Americans, and 10.7% of non-Hispanic Whites were uninsured in 1990. Some 5.3 million of the uninsured had family incomes above $50,000 per year, while an additional 7.2 million had family incomes between $25,000 and $50,000 annually.

Among occupational groups, only judges and legislators had universal coverage. In 1990 the ranks of the uninsured included 29,000 physicians, 18,600 lawyers, 52,500 clergy, 270,000 teachers, 58,000 college professors, and 90,000 engineers.

Hispanics Are Twice as Likely to Lack Health Insurance as Non-Hispanics Whites

UNINSURED HISPANICS

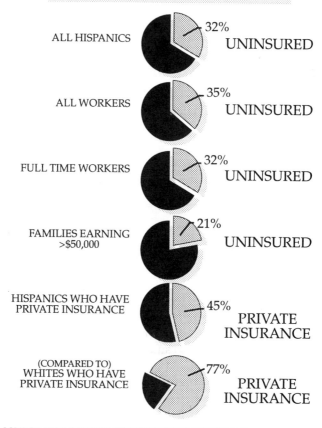

ALL HISPANICS — 32% UNINSURED

ALL WORKERS — 35% UNINSURED

FULL TIME WORKERS — 32% UNINSURED

FAMILIES EARNING >$50,000 — 21% UNINSURED

HISPANICS WHO HAVE PRIVATE INSURANCE — 45% PRIVATE INSURANCE

(COMPARED TO) WHITES WHO HAVE PRIVATE INSURANCE — 77% PRIVATE INSURANCE

SOURCE: HIMMELSTEIN, WOOLHANDLER, WOLFE, 1992
- TABULATIONS FROM CPS

Hispanics are more than twice as likely as non-Hispanic Whites to lack health insurance. Thirty-three percent of all Hispanic-origin Americans are uninsured, including 46% of Mexicanos, 39% of Central and South Americans, 20% of Chicanos, 27% of Mexican-Americans, 21% of Cubans, and 16% of Puerto Ricans. Thirty-five percent of Hispanic men and 29% of Hispanic women are uninsured. Strikingly, 21% of all Hispanics with family incomes above $50,000 per year have no insurance, while 39% of those with family incomes below $25,000 annually are uninsured. Elderly Hispanics are at much greater risk of being uninsured than seniors from other racial and ethnic groups; 5% of Hispanics age 65 and over lack coverage (as compared to 0.9% of all seniors).

Fewer than half of all Hispanics, 45%, have private insurance, compared to 77% of non-Hispanic Whites. Among employed Hispanics, 35% are uninsured, including 33% of all full-time employed Hispanic workers. About 60% of unemployed Hispanic adults are uninsured.

Among the 10 states with the largest Hispanic populations, rates of uninsurance for Hispanic residents in 1990 were: 38.3% in Texas, 37% in California, 35.4% in New Mexico, 34.0% in Florida, 31.1% in Arizona, 26.0% in Colorado, 23.2% in Illinois, 23.1% in New York, 18.2% in New Jersey, and 15.3% in Massachusetts.

1 out of 5
African-Americans Is Uninsured

UNINSURED AFRICAN-AMERICANS

- 21% UNINSURED

- 24% OF ALL WORKERS, AND 20% OF FULL-TIME
  WORKERS ARE UNINSURED

- 16% OF FAMILIES WITH INCOMES OVER $50,000
  ARE UNINSURED

- ONLY 46% HAVE PRIVATE INSURANCE (VS. 78%
  OF ANGLO WHITES)

SOURCE: HIMMELSTEIN, WOOLHANDLER & WOLFE,
1992 - TABULATIONS FROM CPS

African-Americans suffer substantially higher rates of uninsurance than whites. Overall, 21% of African-Americans are uninsured (24% of men and 18% of women). 16% of those with family incomes above $50,000 per year are uninsured, and 24% of those with annual incomes below $25,000 lack coverage. 15% of African-American children and 30% of young adults age 18 to 39 are uninsured.

Only 46% of African-Americans have private insurance, compared to 77% of whites. More than one out of five employed African-Americans is uninsured.

More Money Insures Fewer People

NUMBER OF PEOPLE WITH PRIVATE INSURANCE AND TOTAL INSURANCE PREMIUMS, 1960-1990

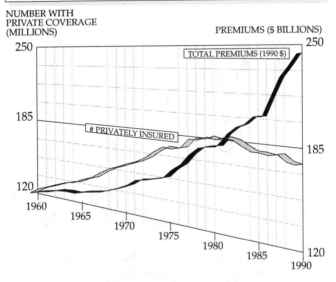

NUMBER WITH
PRIVATE COVERAGE
(MILLIONS)

PREMIUMS ($ BILLIONS)

TOTAL PREMIUMS (1990 $)

PRIVATELY INSURED

SOURCE: HIMMELSTEIN, WOOLHANDLER, WOLFE
- TABULATIONS FROM HIAA/NCHS DATA

From the 1930s until 1980 the number of people with private insurance coverage grew steadily. Since 1980 the number with private coverage has declined. However, the growth of total premiums collected by the private insurance industry has accelerated since 1980.

31

Health Insurance:
Only the Healthy Need Apply

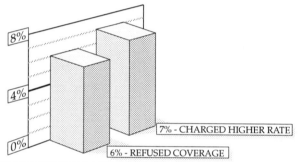

THE MEDICALLY UNINSURABLE

8%

4%

0%

7% - CHARGED HIGHER RATE

6% - REFUSED COVERAGE

SOURCE: LOUIS HARRIS & ASSOC., JANUARY 1990

A Harris Poll found that 6% of Americans had been refused insurance coverage because of past health problems, and 7% had been charged a higher rate for such coverage because of their health history. Past illness strongly predicts high future medical care costs. Hence, insurance companies can minimize future claims by excluding "high risk" enrollees, i.e. those who have been ill in the past.

In the 1987 National Medical Expenditure Survey, uninsured individuals with cardiovascular disease were 5 times as likely, and those with arthritis, rheumatism or hypertension were twice as likely, to have sought but been denied coverage as the average uninsured person. The study found that 3% of those with public coverage (Medicare or Medicaid) had been denied private insurance for medical reasons within the past year.

50 Million *with Insurance* Risk Bankruptcy in the Event of Major Illness

THE **UNDER**-INSURED

Q: HOW MANY PEOPLE HAVE COVERAGE THAT WOULD LEAVE THEM BANKRUPT IN CASE OF A MAJOR ILLNESS?
A: 50 MILLION OR MORE.

Q: HOW MUCH OF SENIORS' BILLS ARE PAID BY MEDICARE?
A: 50%

Q: WHAT PERCENTAGE OF THEIR INCOME DO SENIORS SPEND FOR OUT-OF-POCKET COSTS?
A: >18%, UP FROM 13% TEN YEARS AGO.

Q: HOW MANY YOUNG WOMEN HAVE INSURANCE POLICIES THAT EXCLUDE MATERNITY CARE?
A: 5 MILLION.

SOURCE: SENATE SELECT COMM. ON AGING & ALAN GUTTMACHER INSTITUTE

While at least 35 million Americans have no health insurance, between 50 and 70 million Americans *with* insurance have such inadequate coverage that a major illness would lead to financial ruin.

Insured Americans
Often Can't Afford Care

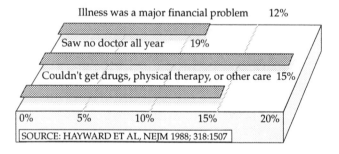

ACCESS PROBLEMS OF **INSURED** AMERICANS
ADULTS AGE <65
WITH SERIOUS OR CHRONIC ILLNESSES

Illness was a major financial problem   12%

Saw no doctor all year   19%

Couldn't get drugs, physical therapy, or other care 15%

0%   5%   10%   15%   20%

SOURCE: HAYWARD ET AL, NEJM 1988; 318:1507

Even those with insurance often face substantial problems in paying for and getting care. According to a 1986 Robert Wood Johnson Foundation survey, 12% of all insured adults under the age of 65 who had a serious or chronic illness experienced a major financial problem due to illness within the last year. Nineteen percent had failed to see a doctor, and 15% were unable to get drugs, physical therapy, or other ancillary services.

Seniors Spend 50% More on Health Costs Than in 1977

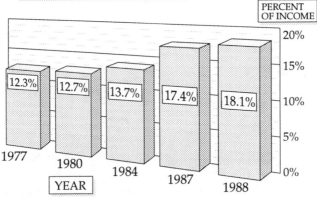

RISING OUT-OF-POCKET HEALTH COSTS FOR SENIORS, 1977-1988

PERCENT OF INCOME

12.3% — 1977
12.7% — 1980
13.7% — 1984
17.4% — 1987
18.1% — 1988

YEAR

20%
15%
10%
5%
0%

SOURCE: SENATE SPECIAL COMMITTEE ON AGING

Because Medicare fails to cover many services such as nursing home care and prescription drugs, and because co-payments and deductibles have been rising even for covered services, the elderly have been forced to spend an increasing proportion of their income on medical care despite Medicare coverage. Medicare currently covers less than half of all medical expenses of the elderly, about the same proportion that was covered by insurance before Medicare was passed. By 1988 the average senior was spending $2,394 annually for medical care bills that were not covered by Medicare—18.1% of total income. This represented a 50% increase in the proportion of income spent by seniors for medical care since 1977.

Avoidance of Care Due to Cost Is on the Rise

PERCENT OF PEOPLE AVOIDING HEALTH CARE
BECAUSE OF COST, 1981 & 1987

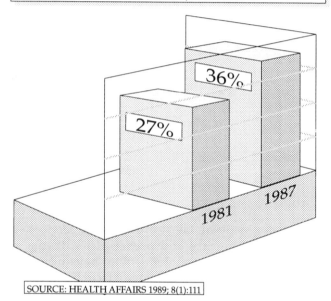

36%

27%

1981

1987

SOURCE: HEALTH AFFAIRS 1989; 8(1):111

Increasing numbers of Americans report avoiding health care because of costs, 27% in 1981 vs. 36% in 1987. In the long run, this may drive up health care costs because early symptoms go untreated, leading in many cases to catastrophic and expensive illnesses. The proportion avoiding care because of costs is nearly three times greater than the proportion uninsured.

More and More People Can't Afford to Pay for Care

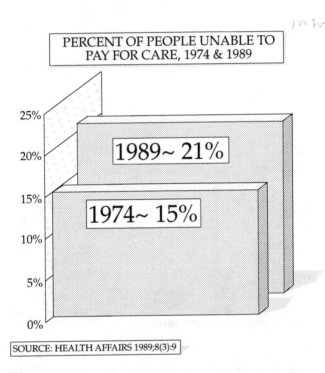

insured?

PERCENT OF PEOPLE UNABLE TO PAY FOR CARE, 1974 & 1989

1989~ 21%

1974~ 15%

SOURCE: HEALTH AFFAIRS 1989;8(3):9

As the costs of health care have risen, more Americans have had difficulty in paying for care. Between 1975 and 1989 there was a 40% increase in those who said they were unable to pay for care. Note that many more people report difficulty in paying for care than report being uninsured.

Employers Cut Their Contribution to Health Costs

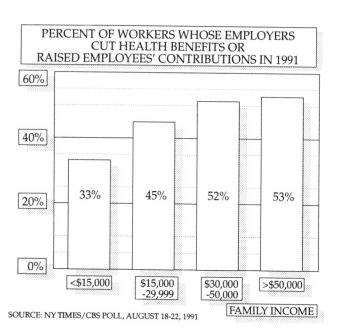

PERCENT OF WORKERS WHOSE EMPLOYERS
CUT HEALTH BENEFITS OR
RAISED EMPLOYEES' CONTRIBUTIONS IN 1991

<$15,000	$15,000-29,999	$30,000-50,000	>$50,000
33%	45%	52%	53%

FAMILY INCOME

SOURCE: NY TIMES/CBS POLL, AUGUST 18-22, 1991

As insurance costs have risen, employers have sought to shift costs onto employees. In 1991, a New York Times poll found that a third of those with family incomes below $15,000, and more than half of those with incomes above $30,000, reported that their employer had increased the employees' contribution or cut their health benefits within the past year.

The Need for Insurance Restricts People's Choices in the Job Market

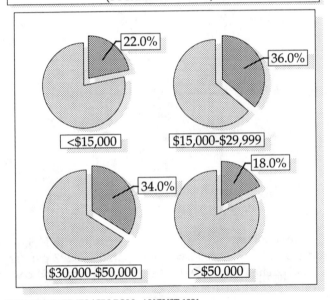

PERCENT OF HOUSEHOLDS WHERE A MEMBER
STAYED AT AN UNWANTED JOB
FOR THE SAKE OF HEALTH COVERAGE
(BY FAMILY INCOME)

22.0%

36.0%

<$15,000

$15,000-$29,999

34.0%

18.0%

$30,000-$50,000

>$50,000

SOURCE: NY TIMES/CBS POLL, AUGUST 1991

Has anyone in your household ever stayed in an unwanted job for the sake of health coverage? While millions of Americans are uninsured and underinsured, tens of millions more stay in unwanted jobs for fear of losing their health insurance coverage.

American Cars Contain More Health Care than Steel

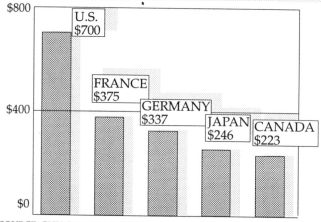

AUTO INDUSTRY HEALTH BENEFIT COSTS
PER CAR, 1988

U.S. $700
FRANCE $375
GERMANY $337
JAPAN $246
CANADA $223

SOURCE: CHRYSLER CORPORATION

In 1988, employee health benefits in the U.S. auto industry cost $700 per car as compared to $223 per car in Canada. The cost of health care now exceeds the cost of steel in American automobiles. It is notable that the U.S. - Canada data compares the cost for the Chrysler Corporation which operates plants in both nations. The skyrocketing costs of health benefits has pushed the leadership of Chrysler to endorse national health insurance.

Health insurance costs are particularly high for older industrial firms such as Chrysler that employ older workers with higher health care costs and also fund health benefits for many retirees.

Corporate Health Spending Skyrockets

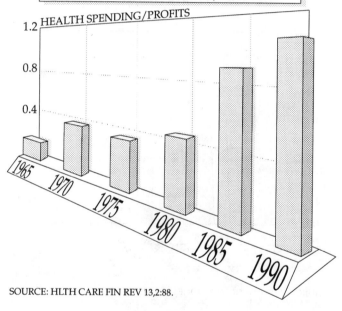

CORPORATE HEALTH SPENDING
COMPARED TO PROFITS, 1965-1990

HEALTH SPENDING/PROFITS

1.2

0.8

0.4

1965 1970 1975 1980 1985 1990

SOURCE: HLTH CARE FIN REV 13,2:88.

Corporate spending for health benefits has risen rapidly over the last 25 years. In 1965 corporations spent 14% as much for health benefits as they retained in profits. By 1990, U.S. corporations were spending more for health benefits than they retained as profits. This increasing cost pressure has led some corporate executives to conclude that a national health program would be beneficial for their corporations.

U.S. Real Wages Decline in Decade of Rapid Economic Growth

DOWNWARD MOBILITY
CHANGE IN REAL WAGES, 1980-1990

PERCENT CHANGE

SOURCE: INTERNATIONAL MONETARY FUND

The U.S. is virtually unique among developed nations in having suffered a decline in real wages during the decade of the 1980s. The decline in U.S. real wages is particularly striking in light of the rapid economic growth that characterized much of the decade. Unfortunately, virtually all of the economic benefits accrued to wealthy individuals.

42

Poverty Is on the Rise

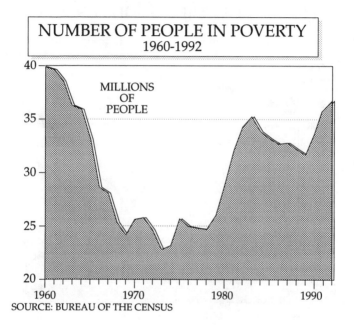

NUMBER OF PEOPLE IN POVERTY
1960-1992

MILLIONS
OF
PEOPLE

SOURCE: BUREAU OF THE CENSUS

The social programs implemented during the 1960s cut poverty rates almost in half. Unfortunately, nearly all of the progress made during the 1960s has been wiped out over the past 15 years. At present, 36.9 million Americans—14.5% of the civilian population—live in poverty.

43

More of Our Children Are Living in Poverty

PERCENT OF CHILDREN IN POVERTY
1960-1992

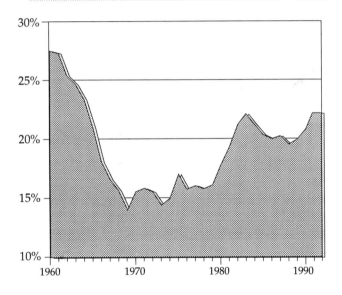

SOURCE: BUREAU OF THE CENSUS

The proportion of American children living in poverty fell steadily during the 1960s from 26.5% in 1960 to 14.9% in 1970. However, since that time the child poverty rate has increased sharply and now stands at 21.9%.

44

U.S. a Leader— in Poverty

POVERTY RATES OF
U.S. & OTHER INDUSTRIALIZED NATIONS, 1986

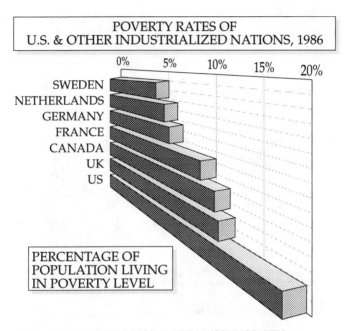

PERCENTAGE OF POPULATION LIVING IN POVERTY LEVEL

SOURCE: LUXEMBOURG INCOME STUDY WORKING PAPERS

The percentage of those living in poverty is much higher in the U.S. than in other wealthy, industrialized nations. The U.S. poverty rate is almost twice as high as that of Canada and the U.K. and four times higher than Sweden's. Since the average income in the U.S. is as high or higher than the average incomes of these other nations, our high poverty rate results from extreme income inequalities.

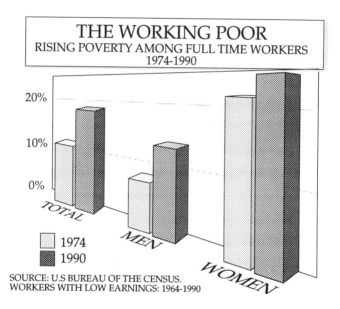

THE WORKING POOR
RISING POVERTY AMONG FULL TIME WORKERS
1974-1990

SOURCE: U.S BUREAU OF THE CENSUS.
WORKERS WITH LOW EARNINGS: 1964-1990

A recent Census Bureau report documented a sharp rise in the proportion of full time, full year (FT/FY) workers with earnings less than the poverty level. Overall, 18% of FT/FY workers earned less than poverty level in 1990, up from 12% in 1974. The figure for men rose from 7.4% to 13.9% (Whites 6.9% to 13.0%, Blacks 13.8% to 22.4%, Hispanics 12.1 to 28.2%). The figure for women rose from 22.1% to 24.3% (Whites 21.8% to 23.6%, Blacks 24.5% to 28.5%, Hispanics 32.6% to 37.0%).

The Rich Get Richer...
While the Poor Get Poorer

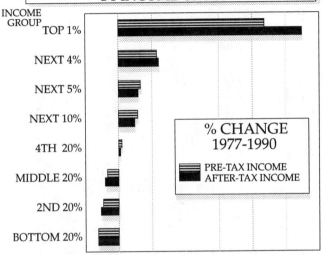

CHANGES IN REAL INCOME 1977-1990
BY INCOME GROUP

SOURCE: CITIZENS FOR TAX JUSTICE, 1990

Since 1977, the wealthiest 1% of the population has gotten substantially richer, while the bottom 60% have actually had a decrease in their real (inflation adjusted) incomes. Pre-tax income increased about 80%, and after-tax income by 110%, for the wealthiest 1%. At the same time, the poorest 20% of the population suffered a 15% loss in real income, and most middle income Americans suffered modest declines as well.

The U.S. Leads the World in CEO/Worker Pay Ratio

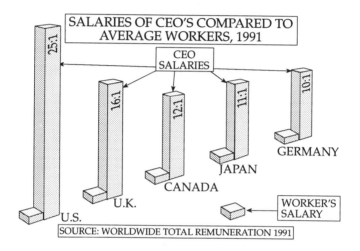

SALARIES OF CEO'S COMPARED TO AVERAGE WORKERS, 1991

CEO SALARIES

25:1 U.S.
16:1 U.K.
12:1 CANADA
11:1 JAPAN
10:1 GERMANY

WORKER'S SALARY

SOURCE: WORLDWIDE TOTAL REMUNERATION 1991

American chief executive officers (CEO's) make about twice as much as their counterparts abroad and twenty-five times more than the average American worker—the largest ratio of any of the 19 major industrial nations. Average total compensation (salary, benefits, stock options, etc.) averages $747,500 in the U.S., $407,600 in Canada, $399,600 in the U.K., $371,800 in Japan, and $364,500 in Germany.

Salary differences are even greater among chief executives at the top 30 companies in the respective nations: $3.2 million in the U.S., $1.1 million in the U.K., $800,000 in Germany, and $500,000 in Japan.

In a Society with a Gold-Plated (but Sorely Lacking) Health System, Other Priorities Are Underfunded

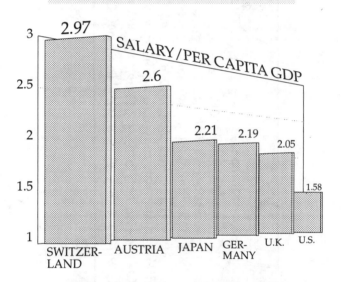

MAXIMUM TEACHER SALARY
COMPARED TO
PER CAPITA GDP, 1988-90

SOURCE: SHAPIRO: WE'RE NUMBER ONE!. NEW YORK, 1992

While the U.S. spends far more for medical care than any other nation, our educational expenditures lag behind most other developed nations.

SYLVIA

by Nicole Hollander

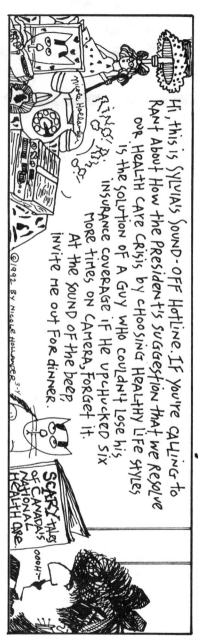

Hi, this is SYLVIA'S Sound-OFF Hotline. IF you're CALLing to RANT ABout How the PResident's Suggestion that we ReSolve OuR HEALTH CaRe CRiSis by cHooSing HEALTHY LIFE Styles is the Solution of A Guy WHo couldN't loSe his INSuRANce coveRAge iF He upcHucked SiX MoRe times on CAMeRA, FoRget it. At the Sound of the beep, INVite me out FoR dinNeR.

RING! RiNg! RiNg!

© 1992 BY NICoLE HoLLANDER 3-4

SCARY tales OF CANADA'S NATIONAL HEALTH care.

OOOOH~

Part II

The Impact of the Crisis:
Care Denied and Delayed

Many uninsured Americans are denied care they desperately need, including emergency care. Prenatal care is often delayed, preventive tests like pap smears are skipped, and vital medicines are unaffordable.

Insurance is critical to good health; without it, people are denied access to care they need, resulting in further illness and sometimes death. Even for many of those with insurance, gaps in their coverage discourage timely care.

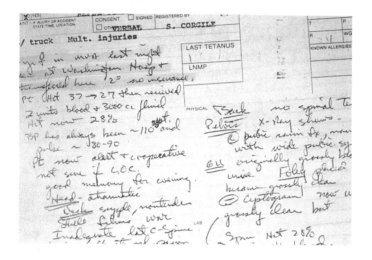

This is the public hospital chart of a patient transferred from a fully equipped private hospital. The chart reads "21 year old female in MVA [motor vehicle accident] seen at Washington Hospital [a private hospital] and transferred here [a public hospital] secondary to no insurance." The chart details how the woman had been hit by a truck, had suffered multiple long bone, pelvic, and rib fractures, and that her hematocrit (blood count) fell from 37% to 28% despite the transfusion of two units of blood (indicating severe internal hemorrhage). Nonetheless, because she failed the "wallet biopsy" (no insurance card found) she was transferred by ambulance nearly 30 miles to a public hospital. After transfer she was noted to have a ruptured aorta (the largest blood vessel in the body). Because the public hospital's chest surgery ser-

52

vice had been closed years earlier because of budget cuts, she was transferred to a third hospital for surgical repair of her aorta.

This case is not unusual. About 300,000 Americans are refused care each year at hospital Emergency Departments because they are uninsured or inadequately insured. A million more are denied care in non-emergent settings. The 1987 National Medical Expenditure Survey found that nearly one million Americans had needed, but did not receive emergency care that year. About half a million Americans reported actually trying, but failing, to get emergency care.

Loss of Coverage Results in Poor Health—and Death

HEALTH EFFECTS OF LOSING INSURANCE IN DIABETICS AND HYPERTENSIVES

- AVERAGE DIASTOLIC BLOOD PRESSURE ROSE FROM 85 TO 95 MM/HG.

- Hgb A1C ROSE FROM 10.2% TO 11.7 %.

- NEITHER BLOOD PRESSURE NOR Hgb A1C ROSE IN THOSE STILL ON MEDICAID.

SOURCE: LURIE NEJM 1984; 311:408

In the early 1980s, California severely curtailed its Medicaid program. Researchers at UCLA followed diabetic and hypertensive patients who lost their Medicaid coverage, and a matched group of patients who remained on the Medicaid rolls. Among those who lost their Medicaid coverage, average blood diastolic pressure rose significantly, and hemoglobin A1C rose from 10.2% to 11.7% indicating deterioration of diabetic control. Neither blood pressure nor diabetic control deteriorated in those who stayed on Medicaid. Several patients suffered severe complications such as strokes, and in some cases even deaths, attributable to their loss of Medicaid coverage.

Delayed Care Increases Death Rates

PATIENTS DELAYING HOSPITAL CARE: BY TYPE OF INSURANCE

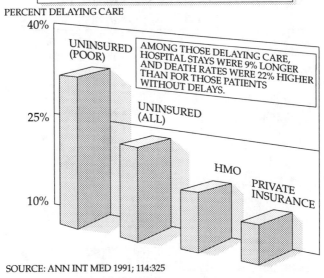

PERCENT DELAYING CARE

40%

UNINSURED (POOR)

AMONG THOSE DELAYING CARE, HOSPITAL STAYS WERE 9% LONGER AND DEATH RATES WERE 22% HIGHER THAN FOR THOSE PATIENTS WITHOUT DELAYS.

UNINSURED (ALL)

25%

HMO

PRIVATE INSURANCE

10%

SOURCE: ANN INT MED 1991; 114:325

Researchers in Massachusetts asked hospitalized patients if their hospitalization had been delayed. The uninsured poor were twice as likely as those with private insurance to report a delay of hospital care, while those with HMO coverage reported slightly more delays than the privately insured. Among those delaying care, hospital stays were longer and death rates higher than for patients without delays, even after adjustment for age and diagnosis.

NUMBER OF PHYSICIAN VISITS
PER YEAR, 1986

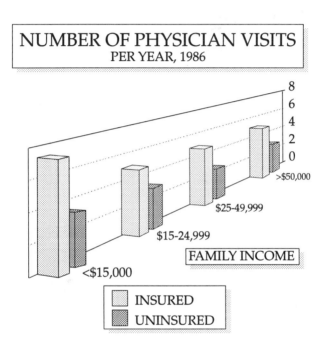

SOURCE: PEPPER COMM/CRS FROM NHIS DATA

Lack of insurance is a strong predictor of failure to get needed medical care. Within each income group, the uninsured are far less likely to have a physician visit than comparable insured persons, according to data from the National Health Interview Survey.

Insured People Get More Hospital Care

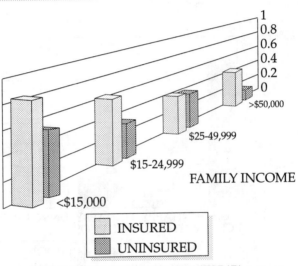

NUMBER OF HOSPITAL DAYS
PER CAPITA BY FAMILY INCOME

INSURED
UNINSURED

SOURCE: PEPPER COMM/CRS FROM NHIS DATA

Lack of insurance is a strong predictor of failure to get needed medical care. Within each income group, the uninsured spend fewer days in the hospital than comparable insured persons, according to data from the National Health Interview Survey.

Poverty and Lack of Insurance Both Decrease Access to Care

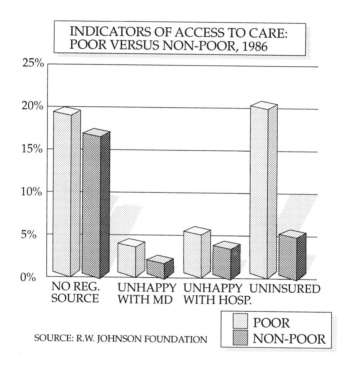

INDICATORS OF ACCESS TO CARE:
POOR VERSUS NON-POOR, 1986

SOURCE: R.W. JOHNSON FOUNDATION

In 1986, the Robert Wood Johnson Foundation commissioned a survey of the United States population regarding their access to medical care. The poor were more likely to be uninsured, were more often unhappy with their physician or hospital care, and were less likely to have a regular source of care.

The Uninsured
Get Less Preventive Care

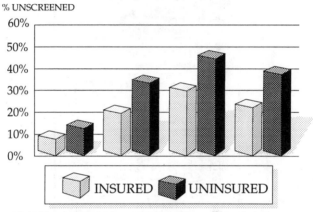

LACK OF PREVENTIVE HEALTH CARE
FOR WOMEN 45-65: INSURED VS. UNINSURED

% UNSCREENED

INSURED   UNINSURED

SOURCE: WOOLHANDLER & HIMMELSTEIN: JAMA 259:2872

In a study published in the Journal of the American Medical Association, lack of health insurance was the most important predictor of failure to received needed preventive services such as blood pressure checks, pap tests, breast examinations, and eye exams. The correlation between lack of health insurance and lack of preventive care was even stronger after multivariate (statistical) control for factors such as race, income and rural residence.

SYLVIA

by Nicole Hollander

THe AMeRICAN MEDICAL ASSOCIATION HAS REJECTED THE IDEA OF A CAP ON HEALTH-CARE SPENDING. THE AMA SAYS THE LIMITS COULD UNDERMINE HEALTH CARE, INTERFERE WITH PATIENT FREEDOM,

AND INHIBIT...

YACHT SALES: —

IN FAMOUS RATIONAL! THING.

©1993 BY NICOLE HOLLANDER

Part III

The Social Costs of the American System: Poor Health Care Leads to Poor Health

We like to view ourselves as the world's greatest nation, yet our health lags behind most other industrialized countries, and even behind some Third World nations. Men in Bangladesh live longer than men in Harlem. Moreover, our health problems and inequities are getting worse.

Fewer Women get
Early Prenatal Care

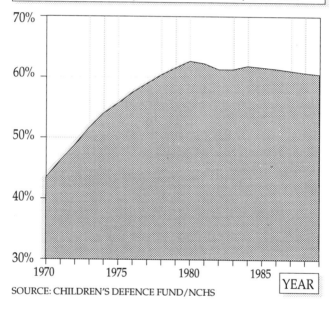

PERCENT OF BLACK WOMEN RECEIVING EARLY
(1ST TRIMESTER) PRENATAL CARE, 1970-1989

SOURCE: CHILDREN'S DEFENCE FUND/NCHS

The proportion of women receiving early (first trimester) prenatal care has actually declined between 1980 and 1989, from 76.3% to 75.5% among all women, and from 62.7% to 60.3% among African-American women. This decline follows decades of steady improvement.

Progress on Black Infant and Child Health Comes to a Standstill

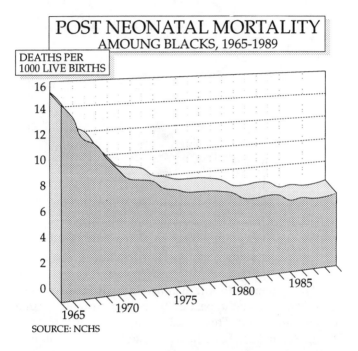

POST NEONATAL MORTALITY
AMOUNG BLACKS, 1965-1989

DEATHS PER
1000 LIVE BIRTHS

16
14
12
10
8
6
4
2
0

1965   1970   1975   1980   1985

SOURCE: NCHS

As access to prenatal care has deteriorated and poverty rates have increased during the past decade, progress on most measures of infant and child health has virtually stopped. For instance, the post neonatal mortality rate for African-Americans, which declined steadily for decades, has shown virtually no improvement over the past decade, and remains far higher than for whites or for residents of most other developed nations.

Black Infant Mortality is *Twice* that of Whites

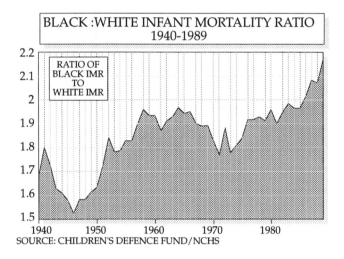

BLACK :WHITE INFANT MORTALITY RATIO
1940-1989

RATIO OF BLACK IMR TO WHITE IMR

SOURCE: CHILDREN'S DEFENCE FUND/NCHS

The black:white infant mortality gap has widened substantially over the past 20 years and currently stands at an all time high. This racial disparity fell precipitously during World War II, coincident with the increase in integration and improved opportunities for African-Americans. This ratio rose again during the 1950s and early 60s. It fell quite sharply in the late 60s and early 1970s, at the time of the landmark civil rights legislation, affirmative action, and implementation of many social programs in response to the civil rights movement. With the retrenchment of the late 70s and the 1980s the racial gap has once again widened, and now stands at the highest level ever recorded.

Many Other Countries Have Lower Infant Mortality Rates that Are Not Influenced by Race

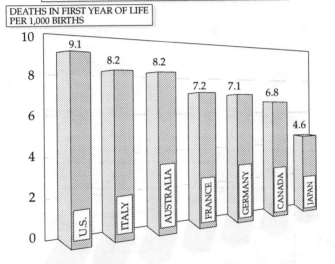

INFANT MORTALITY, 1990

DEATHS IN FIRST YEAR OF LIFE PER 1,000 BIRTHS

U.S.	9.1
ITALY	8.2
AUSTRALIA	8.2
FRANCE	7.2
GERMANY	7.1
CANADA	6.8
JAPAN	4.6

SOURCE: OECD, 1993

The U.S. trails many other nations in infant mortality. Even some developing nations such as Singapore have substantially lower rates of infant death. Moreover, many nations have achieved low infant mortality rates among ethnic and racial minority groups. Thus, infants of non-native-born Swedes (10% of all Swedes) have almost the same low death rates as the infants of native-born Swedes.

Deaths During Pregnancy and Childbirth Are Rising Among African-Americans

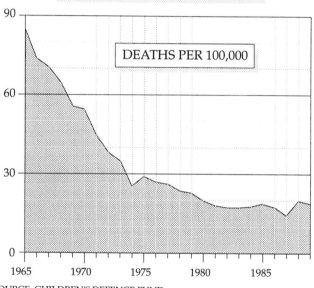

MATERNAL MORTALITY
BLACKS, 1965-1989

DEATHS PER 100,000

SOURCE: CHILDREN'S DEFENCE FUND

The U.S. continues to have a disgracefully high maternal mortality rate (deaths associated with pregnancy and childbirth). Black maternal mortality has actually risen in recent years. This deterioration reflects the declining prenatal care rates during this period and is virtually unprecedented.

Death Rate for African-American Women Stops Declining

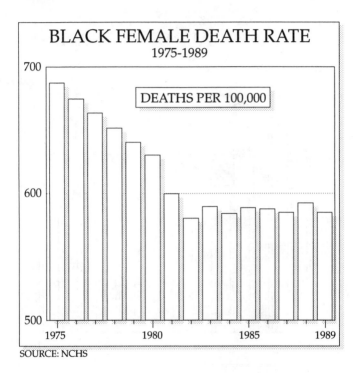

BLACK FEMALE DEATH RATE
1975-1989

DEATHS PER 100,000

700

600

500

1975   1980   1985   1989

SOURCE: NCHS

Over the past decade, as access to medical care has deteriorated and poverty rates have increased, the death rate for Black women has stopped declinig. Such a steady and prolonged deterioration in health status is virtually unprecedented.

African-American Male Death Rate is Increasing

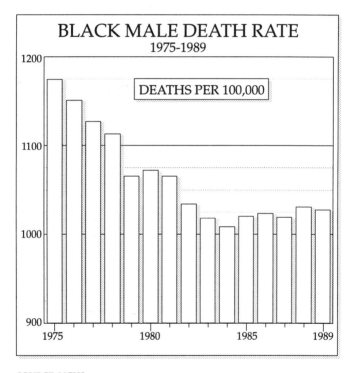

BLACK MALE DEATH RATE
1975-1989

DEATHS PER 100,000

1200

1100

1000

900

1975　　　1980　　　1985　　　1989

SOURCE: NCHS

Over the past decade, as access to medical care has deteriorated and poverty rates have increased, there has been an actual increase in the death rate for Black men.

Men in Harlem Have a Shorter Life Expectancy than Men in Bangladesh

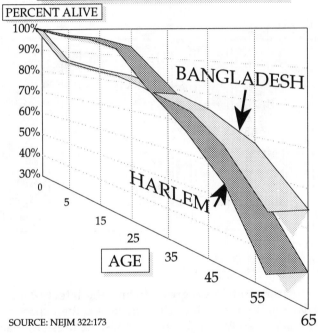

SURVIVAL OF MEN:
HARLEM (U.S.) & BANGLADESH

PERCENT ALIVE

BANGLADESH

HARLEM

AGE

SOURCE: NEJM 322:173

Men living in Harlem now have a shorter average life expectancy than men living in Bangladesh. By the age of 65, only 40% of men in Harlem are still alive, compared to 55% of men in Bangladesh.

White Women Live Nearly Six Years Longer than Black Women

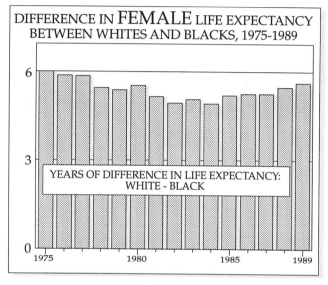

DIFFERENCE IN FEMALE LIFE EXPECTANCY BETWEEN WHITES AND BLACKS, 1975-1989

YEARS OF DIFFERENCE IN LIFE EXPECTANCY: WHITE - BLACK

SOURCE: NCHS

After modest progress during the late 1970s and early 80s, the racial disparities in female life expectancy once again grew during the late 80s. At present, black women die, on average, about 6 years younger than white women. Most of the excess mortality among black women is due to conditions that are highly amenable to medical intervention, such as heart disease, cancer, infant deaths, and diabetes.

White Men Live Nearly Eight Years Longer than Black Men

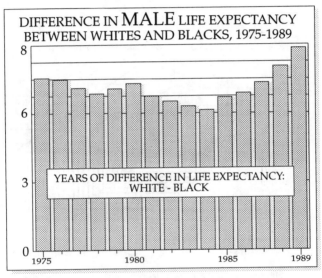

DIFFERENCE IN MALE LIFE EXPECTANCY BETWEEN WHITES AND BLACKS, 1975-1989

YEARS OF DIFFERENCE IN LIFE EXPECTANCY: WHITE - BLACK

SOURCE: STATISTICAL ABSTRACT OF THE U.S./NCHS

The racial disparity in life expectancy declined slowly through the 1970s and early 80s, but this progress was reversed by the mid-80s. At present, black men die about 7 years younger, on average, than white men, and this difference is increasing. Most of this racial disparity is due to diseases highly amenable to medical intervention, such as heart disease (often preventable by treatment of high blood pressure), cancer (in which early detection can be lifesaving), and infant deaths (many preventable by prenatal care).

Life Expectancy Could Be Increased by Better Medical Care

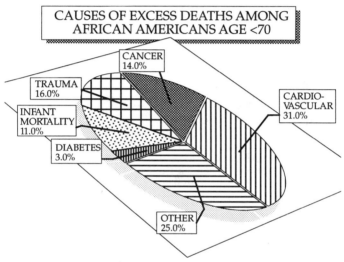

CAUSES OF EXCESS DEATHS AMONG AFRICAN AMERICANS AGE <70

CANCER 14.0%

TRAUMA 16.0%

INFANT MORTALITY 11.0%

DIABETES 3.0%

CARDIO-VASCULAR 31.0%

OTHER 25.0%

SOURCE: SECRETARY'S TASK FORCE ON
BLACK AND MINORITY HEALTH, 1985

Many of the excess deaths among the African-Americans (relative to whites) are due to conditions that are amenable to medical care. Thus, a third of the excess is due to cardiovascular disease, much of that preventable by early blood pressure screening and treatment. Many of the excess cancer deaths are due to inadequate screening and early intervention programs, and much of the infant mortality is clearly preventable with adequate prenatal care.

Poverty and Racism Cause African-Americans' Poor Health

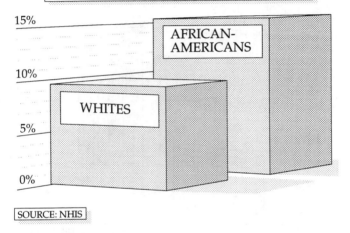

PERCENT OF PEOPLE IN POOR HEALTH BY RACE

AFRICAN-AMERICANS

WHITES

15%

10%

5%

0%

SOURCE: NHIS

African-Americans suffer higher rates of illness than whites. Poverty and racism account for the vast majority of this difference, while genetic factors account for little or none of it. Unfortunately, the U.S. and South Africa share two distinctions in health care. First, we are the only 2 developed nations that do not assure universal access to care. Second, we are the only 2 developed nations that collect detailed health statistics by race but not by income. As a result, we must often use data about the health of African-Americans as a proxy measure of the health of all impoverished Americans.

Wealth
Improves Health

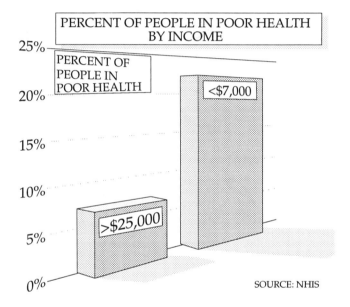

PERCENT OF PEOPLE IN POOR HEALTH
BY INCOME

PERCENT OF PEOPLE IN POOR HEALTH

<$7,000

>$25,000

25%
20%
15%
10%
5%
0%

SOURCE: NHIS

The poor are, on average, in far worse health than the wealthy. Unfortunately, the poor's inadequate access to health care reinforces the damage to health status caused by inadequate housing, food, education, recreational facilities, etc.

Note that a similar pattern of inequality in health status is evident on the chart illustrating the percent of people in poor health by race. The racial inequalities reflect the substantial racial differences in wealth and income, as well as the effects of racism *per se.*

Poverty Correlates with Ill Health

PERCENT OF CHILDREN AGE 5-17 IN EXCELLENT HEALTH, BY FAMILY INCOME, 1986

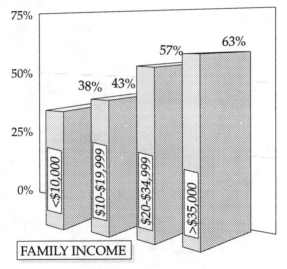

SOURCE: CHILDREN'S DEFENCE FUND, 1989

Wealth is closely correlated with health status. Poor children suffer far higher rates of illness, yet have less access to needed medical care. This pattern epitomizes the Inverse Care Law articulated by the eminent British general practitioner Julian Tudor Hart: "Health care is distributed inversely to need."

American Men Live Shorter Lives

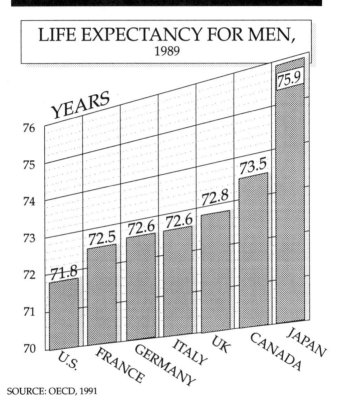

LIFE EXPECTANCY FOR MEN,
1989

YEARS

U.S.	71.8
FRANCE	72.5
GERMANY	72.6
ITALY	72.6
UK	72.8
CANADA	73.5
JAPAN	75.9

SOURCE: OECD, 1991

Life expectancy for men in the U.S. is about 2 years shorter than in several other developed nations, and we trail most other developed countries in this measure of health. Our high poverty rates and lack of access to care are responsible for this poor record on health.

Women Die Younger

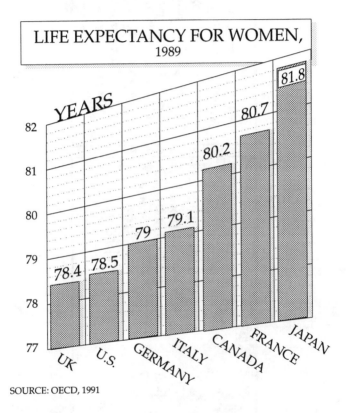

LIFE EXPECTANCY FOR WOMEN,
1989

YEARS

UK	78.4
U.S.	78.5
GERMANY	79
ITALY	79.1
CANADA	80.2
FRANCE	80.7
JAPAN	81.8

SOURCE: OECD, 1991

Life expectancy for women in the U.S. is about 2 years shorter than in several other developed nations, and we trail most other developed countries in this measure of health.

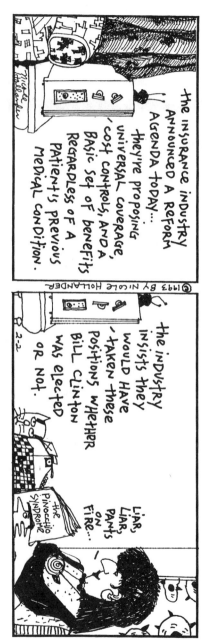

Part IV

Rationing
in the Midst of Plenty

The avoidable suffering documented in the previous section might be an unfortunate necessity in a poor country that couldn't afford better. But while we ration care, we waste billions on unnecessary and even harmful surgery, x-rays, and other medical procedures for the well-insured. A vast army of private-sector bureaucrats, the fastest growing segment of the health care labor force, enforces this inequitable and inefficient pattern of care.

One-Third of Hospital Beds Are Empty While Millions are Denied Needed Care

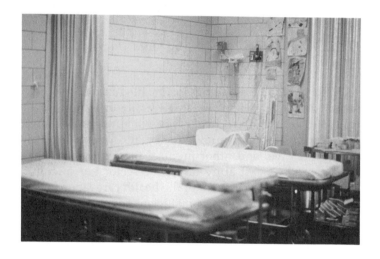

The U.S. currently has a substantial over-supply of hospital beds and other hospital resources. One-third of all hospital beds are empty in this nation, while millions are denied needed care. Moreover, CT scanners, MRI machines, operating rooms, and other expensive equipment often lie idle.

Many High-tech Specialties are Overcrowded

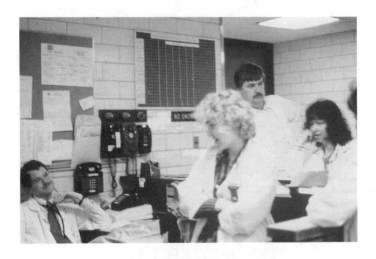

Many analysts foresee a surplus of medical personnel in the United States, and many high technology specialties are already overcrowded.

While Millions Go Without, Many Get Unnecessary Surgery

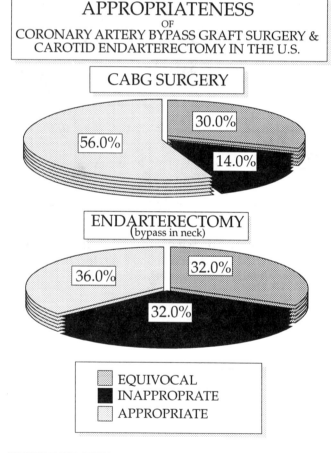

APPROPRIATENESS
OF
CORONARY ARTERY BYPASS GRAFT SURGERY &
CAROTID ENDARTERECTOMY IN THE U.S.

CABG SURGERY

30.0%
56.0%
14.0%

ENDARTERECTOMY
(bypass in neck)

32.0%
36.0%
32.0%

- EQUIVOCAL
- INAPPROPRATE
- APPROPRIATE

SOURCE: RAND CORPORATION, JAMA 260;505 & NEJM 318;721

While we deny needed care to many, we also perform many unnecessary medical procedures that actually worsen health. For instance, a Rand Corporation study found that 14% of coronary artery bypass graft surgeries were clearly inappropriate. Indeed, the study found 6 patients who had normal preoperative coronary angiograms ("clean coronaries") but underwent surgery nonetheless. An additional 30% of coronary artery surgery were for equivocal indications. Only 56% of operations were clearly appropriate. A similar evaluation of carotid endarterectomy yielded even more disturbing results. Little more than one-third of all carotid endarterectomies (operations to bypass blocked blood vessels in the neck) are clearly beneficial to patients.

Other procedures are also performed unnecessarily. About half of all caesarian sections are probably unwarranted, as are many hysterectomies. Substantial numbers of upper GI endoscopies are needlessly performed, as are a variety of other diagnostic tests. A recent review article concluded that about 10% of all operations are unnecessary (Leape LL. Unnecessary surgery. *Annual Review of Public Health* 1992; 13:363-84).

More Technology Isn't Always Better

DUPLICATION OF TECHNOLOGY

HOSPITALS DOING < 200 CARDIOVASCULAR OPERATIONS/YEAR HAVE DEATH RATES (ADJUSTED FOR CASE MIX) 33%-69% HIGHER THAN HIGH VOLUME HOSPITALS.

37/103 CALIFORNIA HOSPITALS PERFORMING HEART SURGERY DID FEWER THAN 150/YEAR. DEATH RATES WERE AS HIGH AS 17.6%.

IN DES MOINES, IOWA (POPULATION 380,000), 2 HOSPITALS DO RENAL TRANSPLANTS WITH 1988 VOLUMES OF 8 & 15 CASES. THE UNIVERSITY HOSPITAL 100 MILES AWAY DID 69 CASES.

SOURCE: HLTH CARE FIN REV 1989 SUPPL. & NEJM 301:1364

In the United States excessive investment in high technology equipment sometimes worsens the quality of care. Research has shown that surgical teams must perform a minimum number of complex procedures each year in order to maintain their competence, and the American College of Surgeons has suggested guidelines for the minimum volume of such procedures that hospitals should perform annually. Yet, more than a third of California hospitals that perform open heart surgery have dangerously low volumes that raise both death rates and costs. Similar patterns of duplicative facilities leading to lower levels of competence and worse patient outcomes are evident for transplants and several other complex surgical procedures. Such duplication also raises costs because each hospital invests in expensive high technology equipment and maintain a full surgical team, whether or not these resources are fully utilized.

Lives Lost Because of Inappropriate Allocation of Resources

MORE FACILITIES, WORSE CARE

ONLY 5 OUT OF 8 DENVER AREA HOSPITALS PERFORMING HEART SURGERY DID AT LEAST 150 CASES IN 1987, THE MINIMUM LEVEL RECOMMENDED BY THE AMERICAN COLLEGE OF SURGEONS TO MAINTAIN COMPETENCE.

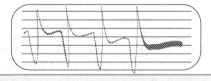

SOURCE:COLORADO HLTH DATA COMM

Denver, like many other cities, has far too many hospitals performing open heart surgery. As a result, 5 of the 8 Denver hospitals that perform heart surgery do too few cases to maintain competence. This both worsens the quality of care and drives costs up due to the expensive duplication of technology. Regionalizing such services would save money and lives.

85

Too Many Machines, Too Much Money, Too Little Care

EXCESS MAMMOGRAPHY MACHINES

- 10,000 MAMMOGRAPHY MACHINES NOW IN THE U.S.

- 2,000 COULD MEET CURRENT DEMAND, AND ONLY 5,132 WOULD BE NEEDED IF ALL WOMEN GOT ALL RECOMMENDED SCREENING TESTS.

- BECAUSE MACHINES ARE UNDERUTILIZED, COST PER TEST IS TWICE AS HIGH AS NECESSARY.

- QUALITY SUFFERS WHEN MAMMOGRAPHERS PERFORM TOO FEW TESTS TO MAINTAIN THEIR COMPETENCE.

SOURCE: ANN INT MED 1990; 113:547

Excessive investment in technology drives up costs and probably drives down quality. At present, there are about 10,000 mammography machines in the U.S. Yet 2,000 could meet all current demand, and about 5,000 would be needed if all women got every recommended mammography test. Hence, most mammography machines lie idle much of the time, and the costs of both machine and staff must be amortized over relatively small numbers of procedures. Paradoxically, the higher costs that result from the excess of mammography machines means that fewer women can afford the test. The quality of testing may also suffer when low volume centers do too few tests to maintain the competence of their operators.

Long Waiting Lines for Emergency Care

Emergency Room (ER) Queues in the U.S. August, 1988

- At the average hospital, on at least one day per month, patients needing intensive care unit (ICU) admission waited more than 15 hours in the ER due to lack if beds.

- Due to overcrowding, the average hospital transferred patients to other facilities on 7% of all days and turned away ambulances on 12% of all days.

- ER crowding and waits for admission were as common at private as at public hospitals.

- In New York City the average hospital's ER was overcrowded on 95% of all days. The wait for an ICU bed was 8 hours, with some hospitals having average waits of 48 hours for a bed.

Source: Andrulis, Ann Emerg Med 1991; 20:980

Denying Care
in the Land of Surplus

RATIONING THE SURPLUS

➤ 1/3 ARE INADEQUATELY INSURED

➤ THEY ARE OFTEN DENIED CARE

➤ THEY ARE SICKER AND DIE YOUNGER

➤ 300,000 EMPTY HOSPITAL BEDS

➤ A GROWING SURPLUS OF PHYSICIANS

➤ MILLIONS OF UNNECESSARY OPERATIONS

While denying needed care to millions, we have substantial, unused medical resources. About 300,000 hospital beds, one-third of the total, lie empty in this country. We face a growing surplus of physicians, and we perform millions of unnecessary procedures and tests. Rationing in the face of a shortage of resources might be a tragic necessity, but rationing in the context of an over supply of resources is morally repugnant.

More Administrators
Keep More Beds Empty

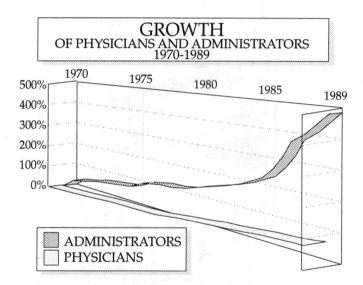

GROWTH
OF PHYSICIANS AND ADMINISTRATORS
1970-1989

SOURCE: STATISTICAL ABSTRACT OF THE U.S. & NCHS

There has been considerable discussion of the growing surplus of physicians in the United States, but little discussion of the surplus of administrators. In fact, administrators are the most rapidly growing segment of the health care labor force. Between 1970 and 1989 the number of health care administrators in the United States increased almost six fold, while the number of physicians (and of other clinical personnel) doubled. It apparently takes substantial administrative effort to keep sick patients out of empty hospital beds.

SYLVIA

by Nicole Hollander

Part V

Exploring the Alternative: Canada's National Health Program

Canada's health care system provides more care for less money. Canadians see their doctors more frequently because they don't have to worry about how much it costs. Far fewer Canadians go without care than do Americans. Canadians even get as many high tech procedures like transplants as do Americans. Most Canadians are happy with their health care system; nine out of ten Americans are dissatisfied with ours. The key to the Canadian success has been universal comprehensive coverage under a single publicly administered health insurance program in each province.

Canada's Plan: *Everyone* Is Covered

MINIMUM STANDARDS
FOR CANADA'S PROVINCIAL PROGRAMS

▶ UNIVERSAL COVERAGE THAT DOES NOT IMPEDE,EITHER DIRECTLY OR INDIRECTLY,WHETHER BY CHARGES OR OTHERWISE, REASONABLE ACCESS.

▶ PORTABILITY OF BENEFITS FROM PROVINCE TO PROVINCE.

▶ COVERAGE OF ALL MEDICALLY NECESSARY SERVICES.

▶ PUBLICLY ADMINISTERED, NON-PROFIT PROGRAM.

Canada's provincial programs must meet four minimum criteria in order to qualify for federal block grants. First, they must enroll virtually everyone in the province, and eliminate essentially all out-of-pocket costs for covered services. Second, benefits must be portable from province to province—that is, if you are from Ontario and get sick in Quebec you must be covered. Third, the provincial program must cover all medically necessary services. The federal government has not defined this requirement further, but all of the provincial programs have enacted comprehensive acute care coverage. There is variability among the provinces in coverage of long term care, dental services, prescription drugs and eye glasses. Fourth, the program must be administered through a public, non-profit agency. This requirement is based on substantial evidence that public administration is far cheaper and more efficient than private insurance administration.

National Health Program Encourages Sick Patients to Visit Doctors

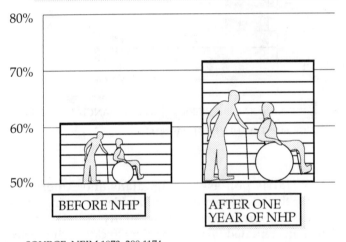

PERCENTAGE OF PEOPLE WITH SERIOUS SYMPTOMS SEEING A DOCTOR BEFORE AND AFTER THE PASSAGE OF NHP IN QUEBEC

BEFORE NHP

AFTER ONE YEAR OF NHP

SOURCE: NEJM 1973; 289:1174

Surveys in Quebec found that within one year of the implementation of the national health program (NHP), the proportion of residents with serious symptoms (such as chest pain, persistent cough, or vomiting blood) who actually saw a physician increased substantially. A variety of other measures confirm that the national health program greatly improved access to care in Canada.

Americans Are 3 Times More Likely than Canadians to Lack Needed Care

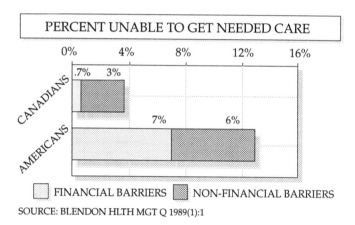

PERCENT UNABLE TO GET NEEDED CARE

CANADIANS: .7% 3%

AMERICANS: 7% 6%

☐ FINANCIAL BARRIERS ▨ NON-FINANCIAL BARRIERS

SOURCE: BLENDON HLTH MGT Q 1989(1):1

A Harris poll asked Canadians and Americans whether they had experienced difficulties in getting needed medical care. Ten times as many Americans as Canadians reported financial barriers to care, a difference that is not surprising since all Canadians are covered by their provincial health insurance program. More surprising is the finding that twice as many Americans as Canadians (6% versus 3%) reported non-financial barriers to care (e.g. queues for services, unavailability of technology, geographic inaccessibility). These data contradict the impression conveyed by the insurance industry and the AMA that medical care is often unavailable or that queues are an important problem in Canada.

Canadians are More Satisfied than Americans

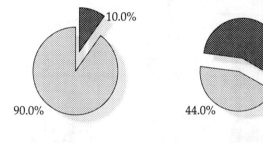

AMERICANS AND CANADIANS
RATE THEIR OWN HEALTH SYSTEMS

AMERICANS — 10.0%, 90.0%

CANADIANS — 56.0%, 44.0%

■ WORKS PRETTY WELL
□ NEEDS BASIC CHANGE

SOURCE: BLENDON HLTH MGT Q 1989 (1):1

A Harris poll asked a random sample of Canadians and Americans to evaluate the health system in their own nation. Ninety percent of Americans said that our system needs basic changes or complete rebuilding. Only 10% thought that the system works pretty well. In contrast, 56% of Canadians said that their system works pretty well.

Canadians Receive More Physician Care than Americans

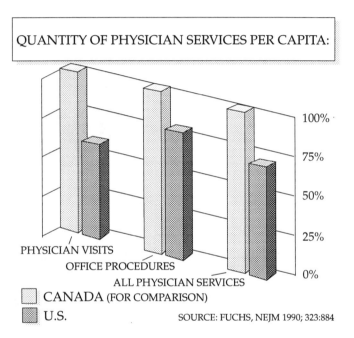

QUANTITY OF PHYSICIAN SERVICES PER CAPITA:

PHYSICIAN VISITS
OFFICE PROCEDURES
ALL PHYSICIAN SERVICES

100%
75%
50%
25%
0%

CANADA (FOR COMPARISON)
U.S.

SOURCE: FUCHS, NEJM 1990; 323:884

The insurance industry and other opponents of a national health program have sought to convey the impression that Canadians' access to care is often restricted. To the contrary, Canadians have substantially more physician visits per capita than do Americans. Moreover, Canadians can go to any doctor or hospital of their choice, while most Americans now have insurance policies that restrict their choice of provider.

Insured Americans Get about as Much Hospital Care as Canadians

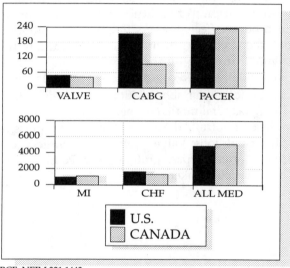

HOSPITAL ADMISSIONS OF ELDERLY FOR CARDIAC DISEASE: U.S vs. CANADA, 1985

SOURCE: NEJM 321:1443

For virtually all cardiac-related diagnoses and interventions, Canadians receive as much care as insured Americans. This study compared elderly Americans covered by Medicare with elderly Canadians. Hospital admission rates for both medical and surgical care were comparable with the single exception of coronary artery bypass graft surgery. This procedure is almost certainly over-used in the U.S.

Queues for coronary artery surgery developed in some provinces in Canada during the mid and late 1980s, largely because many Canadian coronary care nurses and bypass pump technicians were attracted by bonuses offered by U.S. hospitals expanding their programs. In some areas, patients waited on long queues for a particular surgeon, while other surgeons across town (or even in the same hospital) had little or no queue. The queues, which never affected access to emergency surgery, have now been reduced in most areas of Canada through expanded funding by the provincial single payer programs and improved coordination of referral networks.

The following abbreviations are used in this chart: MI = myocardial infarction (heart attack); CHF = congestive heart failure; All Med = all medical admissions for cardiac conditions; Valve = heart valve surgery; CABG = coronary artery bypass graft surgery; Pacer = placement of a cardiac pacemaker.

Transplants Are As Available in Canada as in the U.S.

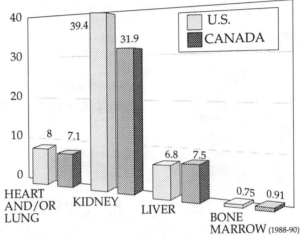

TRANSPLANTS:
U.S AND CANADA, 1990

TRANSPLANTS PER 100,000 POPULATION

Legend: U.S. / CANADA

HEART AND/OR LUNG: 8 / 7.1
KIDNEY: 39.4 / 31.9
LIVER: 6.8 / 7.5
BONE MARROW (1988-90): 0.75 / 0.91

SOURCE: OECD 1993 & ANN INT MED 1992; 116:507
NOTE: DATA FOR HEART/LUNG IN CANADA ARE FROM 1989;
FOR LIVER IN U.S., 1988

Opponents of a single payer system have asserted that high technology care is unavailable in Canada. In fact, compared to Americans, Canadians have comparable rates of heart and/or lung, liver, bone marrow transplants, and kidney transplants.

Canada has regionalized most of these services. A relatively small number of centers each perform a large number of procedures. Such regionalization improves the quality of care since high volume centers are better able to maintain competence, and minimizes cost by avoiding the unnecessary duplication of expensive facilities.

Faster Care In Canada
for Breast Cancer Patients

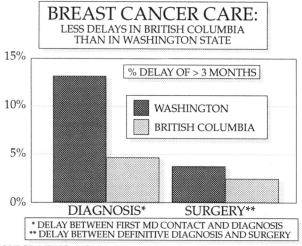

BREAST CANCER CARE:
LESS DELAYS IN BRITISH COLUMBIA
THAN IN WASHINGTON STATE

% DELAY OF > 3 MONTHS

WASHINGTON
BRITISH COLUMBIA

DIAGNOSIS*   SURGERY**

* DELAY BETWEEN FIRST MD CONTACT AND DIAGNOSIS
** DELAY BETWEEN DEFINITIVE DIAGNOSIS AND SURGERY

SOURCE: MEDICAL CARE 1993; 34:264

The U.S. media has prominently reported anecdotes of waits for care in Canada. However, this systematic study of waits in breast cancer care found that Canadians received more timely care. Fewer Canadian women waited more than three months between their first contact with a physician for breast symptoms and a definitive diagnosis of their breast cancer. Canadian women were also slightly less likely to experience a prolonged delay between the time of diagnosis and surgery.

Americans
See Their Doctors Less Often

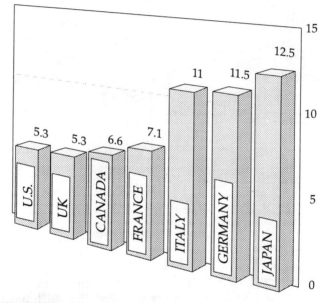

PHYSICIAN VISITS PER CAPITA, 1988

- U.S. — 5.3
- UK — 5.3
- CANADA — 6.6
- FRANCE — 7.1
- ITALY — 11
- GERMANY — 11.5
- JAPAN — 12.5

SOURCE: OECD, 1993
NOTE: DATA FOR GERMANY ARE FROM 1987

Americans have about the same physician visits per capita as the British and Canadians, and only half as many physician visits as Italians, Germans, or Japanese. Yet all of these nations have much lower health care costs than the U.S.

Americans Get Less Health Care as Measured by Length of Hospital Stay

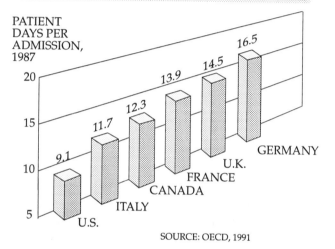

AVERAGE LENGTH OF STAY IN HOSPITAL

PATIENT DAYS PER ADMISSION, 1987

SOURCE: OECD, 1991

Many U.S. health policy leaders blame rising health costs on the American people for using too much health care, and base their cost containment strategies on limiting the delivery of services through detailed utilization review and managed care bureaucracies. However, for most types of services Americans get less health care than people in many other nations with lower health expenditures. For instance, the average length of stay in hospital is 20 to 40 percent shorter in the U.S. than in most other developed nations.

Canada's Plan
Provides Safer Surgery

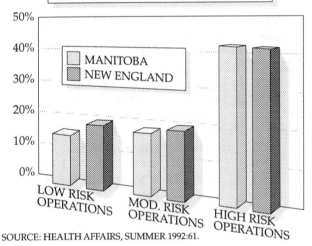

SURGICAL MORTALITY
AT THREE YEARS FOR THE ELDERLY:
MANITOBA VS. NEW ENGLAND

MANITOBA
NEW ENGLAND

LOW RISK OPERATIONS
MOD. RISK OPERATIONS
HIGH RISK OPERATIONS

SOURCE: HEALTH AFFAIRS, SUMMER 1992:61.

There is no credible evidence of better quality care in the U.S. than in Canada. Yet the insurance industry and other opponents of a Canadian-style national health program have publicized allegations that the quality of care in Canada is lower than in the U.S. As stated in the editor's introduction to the article reporting the data shown in the graph above: "The Bush health plan misinterpreted earlier research on surgical outcomes in New England and Manitoba, emphasizing that 'post-operative mortality . . . is 44% higher in Canada than in the U.S. for high risk procedures.' As this paper shows, much of the short-term mortality differential is explained by the special problems of transferring hip fracture patients in sparsely populated Manitoba. The overall findings are dramatically different. Adjusting for case-mix, long-term survival after 9 of 10 procedures in fact favors Manitoba over New England."

Canadians, as compared to Americans, have a longer life expectancy at birth (males 73.7 vs. 71.6; females 80.6 vs. 78.6), longer life expectancy at age 65 (males 16.3 vs. 16; females 19.8 vs. 18.9), lower infant mortality (7 vs. 10 per thousand births), lower maternal mortality (7 vs. 13 per 100,000) and lower under-5 mortality (8 vs. 13 per thousand). Canadians get more hospital admissions (136 vs. 126 per 1000 inhabitants) and hospital days (1468 vs. 910 per 1000 population), more physician visits (6.6 vs. 5.3 per capita), more immunizations (85% vs. 45% of one-year-olds fully immunized), and more surgical procedures (110 vs. 88 per 1000 population), but fewer C-sections (19.5% vs. 24.7% of births—probably too high in both nations).

Surgery in Canada Is Not Biased Toward Higher Incomes

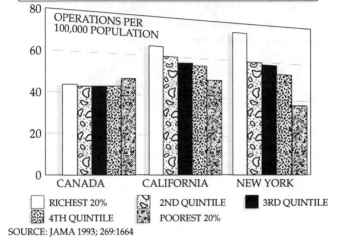

CABG RATES FOR THE NON-ELDERLY
BY INCOME QUINTILE:
CANADA, CALIFORNIA, AND NEW YORK

OPERATIONS PER 100,000 POPULATION

CANADA   CALIFORNIA   NEW YORK

| | RICHEST 20% | | 2ND QUINTILE | | 3RD QUINTILE |
| | 4TH QUINTILE | | POOREST 20% |

SOURCE: JAMA 1993; 269:1664

There has been much attention devoted to lower rates of coronary artery bypass graft surgery (CABG) in Canada than in the U.S. (The widely publicized waits for CABG in some Canadian cities in the late 1980s have now virtually disappeared). The study cited above confirms the difference in the two nations' CABG rates. While it is not clear whether the U.S. rate is too high or the Canadian rate is too low, Canada has a lower age-adjusted death rate from ischemic heart disease than does the U.S. (males 241.5 vs. 254.9; females 117.8 vs. 137.9 per 100,000 population). Moreover, there is evidence that our more invasive treatment style does not improve death rates or prevent heart attacks (see next chart).

In Canada, patients under 65 living in poorer neighborhoods are more likely to undergo CABG. This pattern is clinically appropriate, since coronary artery disease is more prevalent among the poor. In contrast, in the U.S. wealthier populations (with lower disease prevalence) are more likely to undergo CABG. This finding suggests that care is distributed according to need in Canada, and according to ability to pay in the U.S.

More High-Tech Care in the U.S. Does Not Save Lives

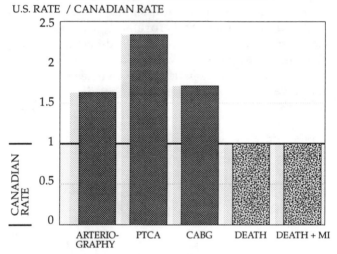

ACUTE MI
(HEART ATTACK)
U.S. VS. CANADA

U.S. RATE / CANADIAN RATE

SOURCE: "SAVE" STUDY, NEJM 1993; 328:779

This chart shows data from a randomized trial that enrolled patients with MIs (heart attacks) from 93 hospitals in the U.S. and 19 hospitals in Canada. Half the patients in each country received the drug captopril, and the other half placebo. Otherwise, treatment was chosen by the doctor and patient, and presumably represents the usual care and outcomes across a broad cross-section of each nation.

Seventy-eight percent of the 1573 U.S. patients underwent coronary arteriography, compared to 48% of the 658 Canadian patients. Americans were 2.33 times more likely to undergo percutaneous transluminal angioplasty (PTCA), and 1.71 times as likely to undergo coronary artery bypass graft surgery (CABG). Yet, rates of death and recurrent MI were no different in the two nations. Anginal chest pain was slightly more common in Canadian patients both before and after their heart attacks (6% difference before MI, 5% difference one year after MI, 6% difference 2 years after MI). Overall, this study found that U.S. patients were subjected to many more invasive tests and operations, but derived little or no benefit.

Canada's System
Doesn't Compromise Innovation

RESEARCH OUTPUT 1990

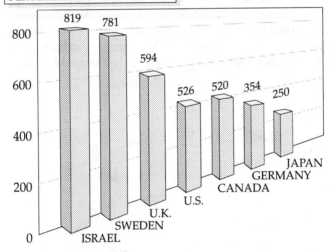

MEDICAL ARTICLES PUBLISHED
PER MILLION POPULATION

ISRAEL 819
SWEDEN 781
U.K. 594
U.S. 526
CANADA 520
GERMANY 354
JAPAN 250

SOURCE: LANCET 1993; i:247

Opponents of a National Health Program often argue that such reform would compromise innovation in U.S. health care. There is no evidence to support this argument. The overwhelming majority of basic bio-medical research is supported by grants from government or non-profit foundations. Often, as in the case of the HIV drug AZT, the results of government funded basic research are turned over to drug firms who do minimal additional scientific work, but reap rich rewards. Drug and equipment firms spend more for marketing than for research, and may label as "research" some marketing activities. Moreover, much drug industry research focuses on developing so-called me-too drugs that offer no clinical advantage over existing medications, but yield a chemically distinct, and hence patentable, version of an older drug.

We are unaware of systematic international comparisons of research productivity. However, the limited data reproduced on this chart does not support the view that the U.S. research establishment is more productive than researchers in nations with national health programs.

U.S. Physician Income Is Higher for Specialists but Not for Primary Care Doctors

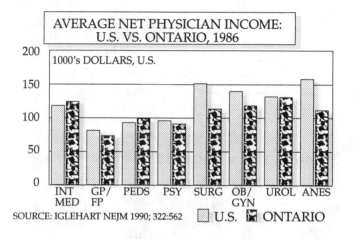

AVERAGE NET PHYSICIAN INCOME: U.S. VS. ONTARIO, 1986

1000's DOLLARS, U.S.

INT MED · GP/FP · PEDS · PSY · SURG · OB/GYN · UROL · ANES

SOURCE: IGLEHART NEJM 1990; 322:562 · U.S. · ONTARIO

Primary care physicians earn similar incomes in the U.S. and Canada. Procedure-oriented specialists earn somewhat more in the U.S. than in Canada. Mean physician income is also higher in the U.S. than in Canada, in part because the physician mix in the U.S. is more heavily weighted towards highly paid specialists, while half of all physicians in Canada are primary care practitioners who are paid less in both nations.

Physicians' incomes in Canada have risen at almost exactly the same rate as inflation since implementation of the NHP.

The figures given in this chart are for physician net incomes after deducting practice expenses, but before taxes.

111

Nursing Salaries Similar in U.S. and Canada

AVERAGE NURSING SALARIES:
U.S. & CANADA, 1986 (IN PPP $)

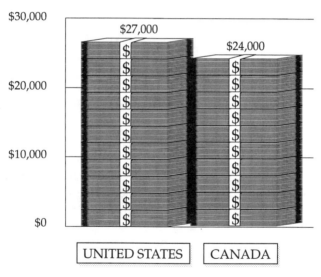

SOURCE: OECD 1991

Nursing incomes, and incomes of other non-physician health care personnel, are similar in the U.S. and in Canada. (The currency conversion used in this chart is based on purchasing power parities.)

German System Is No Answer: It Saves by Paying Workers Poorly

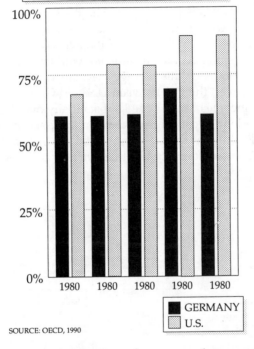

HEALTH WORKERS' EARNINGS
AS A PERCENT OF
AVERAGE EARNINGS:
GERMANY & U.S., 1970-1989

GERMANY
U.S.

Supporters of an employer mandate approach to health care reform often laud the German health care system as an example of a multiple payer system that provides almost universal access to care, yet effectively contains costs. Unfortunately, since the German system is as administratively complex as U.S. health care, savings have had to be derived from clinical areas. Physicians' incomes have remained quite high, spending on high technology has been only slightly lower than U.S. levels, and spending for pharmaceuticals is even higher than in the U.S. However, spending for health workers' wages is far lower than in the U.S. or Canada.

In addition to employing many fewer non-physician health care workers than in the U.S., the German system pays them lower wages. Whereas the average health care worker in the U.S. makes 90% of the average wage of all U.S. workers, the average health care worker in Germany makes only 60% of the average German worker's earnings. Moreover, the gap between U.S. and German health workers' incomes has widened substantially over the past 20 years. Hence, cost control based on the German model would require that the U.S. employ far fewer health care workers and pay them far less than we now do.

Canada Saves on Administration but Doesn't Skimp on Caregivers

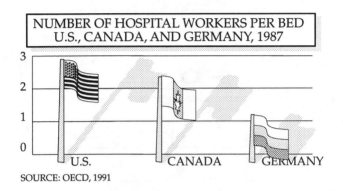

**NUMBER OF HOSPITAL WORKERS PER BED
U.S., CANADA, AND GERMANY, 1987**

SOURCE: OECD, 1991

This chart depicts the number of hospital workers per hospital bed in the U.S., Canada, and Germany. The U.S. and Canadian figures are quite similar, 2.95 in the U.S. and 2.45 in Canada, but the German figure is far lower, 1.25 workers per bed. Since all 3 nations have similar numbers of beds per capita, Germany employs far fewer hospital workers per capita than the U.S. or Canada. It is notable that all 3 nations have a similar number of physicians per capita, so the difference in the number of hospital workers is indicative of a substantially lower number of non-physician personnel in German hospitals.

In contrast to the Canadian single-payer system which has cut costs mainly by streamlining administration and regionalizing some high technology services, the German system has economized largely by cutting back on nurses and other non-physician health personnel.

Respect for Medical Profession is Higher in Canada than in the U.S.

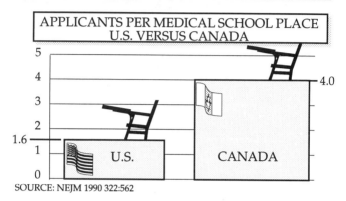

APPLICANTS PER MEDICAL SCHOOL PLACE
U.S. VERSUS CANADA

SOURCE: NEJM 1990 322:562

During the 1980s the number of people applying to medical school in the U.S. declined dramatically (though applications appear to be rebounding in the early 1990s), while Canada experienced no such decline. Medicine remains a popular and respected profession in Canada. Polls indicate that Canadian physicians believe that the national health program has improved the health of the population, and provides a good practice environment and lifestyle for physicians. In contrast, physician dissatisfaction has increased dramatically in the U.S. over the past 20 years.

Part of the U.S.-Canada differential in medical school applicants is due to the far lower tuition charged by Canadian schools. The Canadian government has recognized that the cost of medical education is an integral part of the overall costs of medical care. It has chosen to subsidize medical schools and keep tuition low (about $2000 per year) rather than bearing the costs retrospectively through higher physicians' incomes required to pay back medical school loans.

Canadians Are Most Satisfied with Care— Americans Least Satisfied

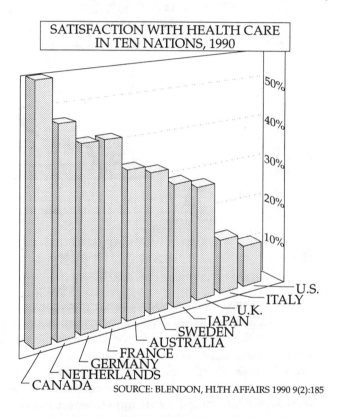

SATISFACTION WITH HEALTH CARE
IN TEN NATIONS, 1990

50%
40%
30%
20%
10%

U.S.
ITALY
U.K.
JAPAN
SWEDEN
AUSTRALIA
FRANCE
GERMANY
NETHERLANDS
CANADA

SOURCE: BLENDON, HLTH AFFAIRS 1990 9(2):185

The Harris polling organization surveyed random samples of the population in each of 10 industrialized nations. Canadians were most satisfied with their care, while America trailed all the other nations.

Canada's Health Care System Costs Less than Ours

HEALTH COSTS AS % OF GNP:
U.S. & CANADA, 1960-1991

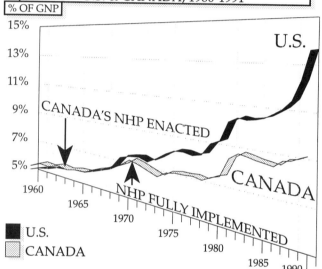

SOURCE: STATISTICS CANADA & NCHS/COMMERCE DEPARTMENT

The main argument used against national health insurance in the early 1970s was that we could not afford it. We now have clear evidence that a national health program is the most effective means of cost containment. U.S. and Canadian health care costs, as a percent of GNP, were almost identical until the full implementation of the Canadian national health program in 1971. Since that time, Canadian costs have leveled off at about 9% of GNP, while U.S. costs have increased to 14% of GNP, and continue to rise.

A single payer system facilitates cost containment in three ways. First, it can achieve substantial administrative

118

savings that are not attainable under a multi-payer system. Second, the single payer is easily able to set and enforce overall budgetary limits. Effectively limiting the overall health budget is extremely difficult under our multiple payer system with 1,200 different private insurers, and more than 200 million Americans paying health bills. Finally, a single payer system facilitates health planning to eliminate duplication of facilities and expensive technology that often wastes money and sometimes worsens quality. For instance, U.S. hospitals average only 65% occupancy; we have 10,000 mammography machines when only 5,000 would be needed to perform every test recommended for every woman in the nation. So many hospitals perform open heart surgery that many do too few procedures to maintain their competence.

The insurance industry has sponsored studies claiming that health costs are rising as rapidly in Canada as in the U.S. This claim is based on a time period carefully selected to be unfavorable to Canada's system and uses for actual health spending rather than health spending's share of GNP. However, the raw health spending comparisons are greatly affected by exchange rate fluctuations and do not take into account differences between nations in changes in real wages and incomes. Since real wages have gone up rapidly in Canada but not in the U.S., Canada's rising overall wage level has pushed up the wage bill for hospitals and other health care providers.

As a result, health costs have risen but care is no less affordable for the average Canadian. In contrast, health care costs increases in the U.S. have far exceeded increases in average income, making care less affordable. For this reason, almost all health economists agree that international comparisons of health care costs should rely on the proportion of GNP (or GDP) spent on care.

Part VI

Why Our System Costs More and Delivers Less: Administrative Waste in U.S. Health Care

Eliminating insurance companies' overhead, and the morass of paperwork inflicted on American patients, doctors and hospitals by our 1200 private health insurers, would save enough money to cover the uninsured, and to improve coverage for many who currently have insurance. Americans pay more for less in a wasteful and inefficient system. Health insurance companies invoke Americans' distaste for big government to rally opposition to national health insurance. But our private health insurers are far less efficient than Canada's government-run insurance programs. Moreover, American patients and doctors suffer insurance company intrusions and dictates that no Canadian would tolerate.

Several explanations for the fast rise in health care costs are false: the proportion of Medicare spending for patients in the last year of life has not risen; care for HIV patients, while it may be expensive, is a negligible one percent of total health care costs; and illegal drug abuse is not a major cost—less than one percent of emergency room visits involve an illegal drug-related incident.

More Money in Canada Devoted to Care Instead of Overhead

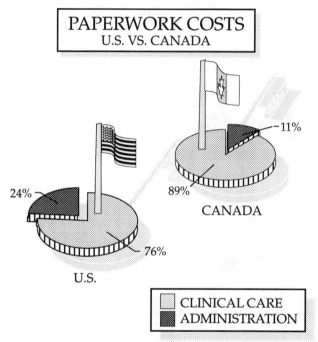

PAPERWORK COSTS
U.S. VS. CANADA

11%
24%
89%
76%
CANADA
U.S.

CLINICAL CARE
ADMINISTRATION

SOURCE: WOOLHANDLER & HIMMELSTEIN NEJM 1991; 324:1253

In 1987, 24% of total U.S. health spending went for administration compared to 11% in Canada. Moreover, since total health spending was 40% higher in the U.S. than in Canada, the 13% difference in administration probably understates the real difference.

Americans Pay 6 Times More for Insurance Overhead than Canadians

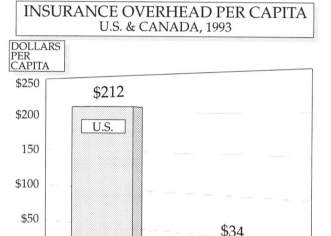

INSURANCE OVERHEAD PER CAPITA
U.S. & CANADA, 1993

DOLLARS PER CAPITA

$212 — U.S.

$34 — CANADA

SOURCE: WOOLHANDLER/HIMMELSTEIN NEJM 1991; 324:1253, UPDATED 1993

A single payer system greatly streamlines insurance administration. Insurance company advertising and sales costs are almost completely eliminated, since everyone is automatically enrolled under the universal program. The government single payer can use the existing tax collecting agencies to garner funds with little additional administrative costs, unlike insurance companies which must maintain extensive premium collection bureaucracies.

Paying health care bills is also far simpler for a single payment agency than for the multiple insurers. Hospitals can be paid a lump sum budget rather than on a per-service or per-patient basis, eliminating hundreds of millions of bills each year. Moreover, extensive insurance company efforts to shift costs onto other payers are eliminated since the single payer is responsible for virtually all bills. As a result, insurance overhead cost $178 per person less in Canada than in the United States in 1993.

In 1990, Blue Cross/Blue Shield of Massachusetts employed more than 6600 people to administer insurance to two and a half million New England residents. In contrast, 435 people work for British Columbia's provincial plan which covers 3.1 million residents. More people work for Blue Cross/Blue Shield of Massachusetts than work administering Canada's National Health Program that covers 26 million people.

U.S. Insurance Overhead Is Enormous; Canada's Is Negligible

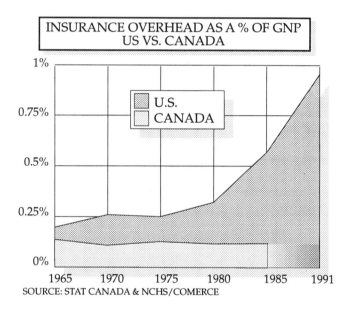

INSURANCE OVERHEAD AS A % OF GNP
US VS. CANADA

SOURCE: STAT CANADA & NCHS/COMERCE

Health insurance overhead alone now accounts for almost 1% of Gross National Product (GNP) in the U.S., as compared to about 0.1% of GNP in Canada. U.S. private insurers keep, on average, 14% of total premium dollars for their overhead and profits. That is, for every dollar of premium paid, 14¢ stays with the insurance company and 86¢ goes towards clinical care. Total insurance overhead in the U.S. will approach $50 billion in 1993. Canada's provincial health insurance plans run for an overhead of less than 1% of total costs.

Multiple Payers Are Less Efficient than a Single Payer Plan

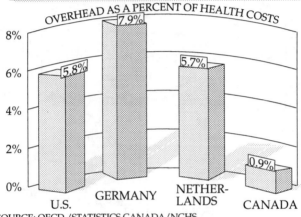

INSURANCE OVERHEAD, 1990:
U.S., GERMANY, NETHERLANDS, & CANADA

OVERHEAD AS A PERCENT OF HEALTH COSTS

- U.S.: 5.8%
- GERMANY: 7.9%
- NETHERLANDS: 5.7%
- CANADA: 0.9%

SOURCE: OECD /STATISTICS CANADA/NCHS

The costs of insurance overhead are uniformly higher in nations with multi-payer insurance systems than under single payer systems. Both Germany and the Netherlands have multi-payer systems that have been touted as potential models for the U.S. Insurance overhead costs in both nations are comparable or slightly higher than costs in the U.S. because of the administrative complexity inherent in multiple payer schemes. Canada's costs are far lower, as are insurance overhead costs in other nations with single payer systems, eg. Sweden, the United Kingdom, and Australia.

125

Competition
Raises Hospital Costs

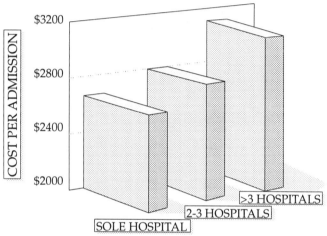

SOURCE: WALL STREET JOURNAL, 4/90

In medical care increased competition may actually worsen efficiency and raise costs. Hospitals often compete not by improving quality or lowering prices, but by engaging in a medical "arms-race". This results in wasteful duplication of expensive technology as each hospital seeks to offer the latest high-tech gadgetry. A study published in the Wall Street Journal in 1990 found that hospitals in more competitive markets actually had substantially higher costs than hospitals facing less competition.

Insurance Overhead: Many Components Are Eliminated in the Canadian System

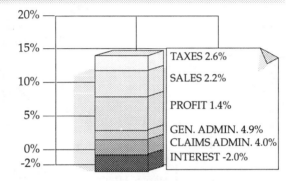

COMPONENTS OF PRIVATE INSURANCE OVERHEAD

TAXES 2.6%
SALES 2.2%
PROFIT 1.4%
GEN. ADMIN. 4.9%
CLAIMS ADMIN. 4.0%
INTEREST -2.0%

SOURCE: CURTIS, HEALTH MANAGEMENT Q 1991;(4):6

This chart displays a breakdown of the various components of insurance overhead. "Claims administration" (4% of total premium) is the administrative cost of paying claims. "General administration" (4.9% of total premiums) includes the cost of collecting premiums. Advertising, commissions, and other sales costs are included under the rubric "sales." Insurance companies derive interest income from investing the money they collect in premiums before they pay it out as claims. This is shown as a negative number on the chart since it actually adds to insurance company revenues, i.e. is a negative cost. The interest credit, which is not included in most estimates of private health insurance overhead, approximately offsets taxes, which are included.

Health Maintenance Organizations Don't Cut Out the Waste

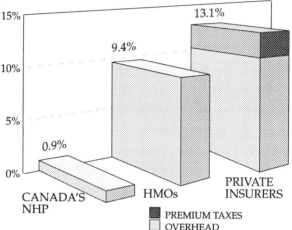

INSURANCE OVERHEAD:
HMOs, PRIVATE INSURERS & CANADA'S NHP.

SOURCE: GHAA/HIAA (excludes 2% interest credit) & STATISTICS CANADA

The administrative costs of HMOs are comparable to those of other private insurers, and are far higher than those of a single payer system. Nationwide, HMO overhead averaged 9.4% of total premiums in 1990, compared to the 13.1% overhead of other private insurance programs. However, most of this difference is accounted for by premium taxes, paid by private insurance companies, but not HMO's. The overhead costs for both HMOs and private insurance should be corrected upward for an interest credit, i.e. the money earned by investing premiums before claims are paid. Even excluding these investment earnings, both HMOs and indemnity insurers in the U.S. have overhead rates 10 times higher than Canada's national health program.

What the Bureaucracy Is Paid For: Oversee, Push Paper, and Sell, Sell, Sell

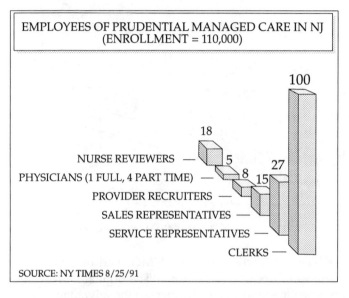

EMPLOYEES OF PRUDENTIAL MANAGED CARE IN NJ
(ENROLLMENT = 110,000)

100

18

NURSE REVIEWERS — 5

27

PHYSICIANS (1 FULL, 4 PART TIME) — 8 15

PROVIDER RECRUITERS —

SALES REPRESENTATIVES —

SERVICE REPRESENTATIVES —

CLERKS —

SOURCE: NY TIMES 8/25/91

Policymakers increasingly advocate managed care, with stringent bureaucratic control of clinical practice, as the solution to rising health care costs. Yet managed care bureaucracies are themselves expensive. A single managed care program in New Jersey that covered 110,000 enrollees employed almost 200 full time administrative and utilization review personnel (about as many as work for a typical Canadian provincial health insurer covering one and a half million provincial residents). Note that the figures given on the chart exclude the staff at insurance agencies that sell this managed care plan, as well as the staff at the head offices of the Prudential Corporation.

Profit: a Growing Factor in HMOs

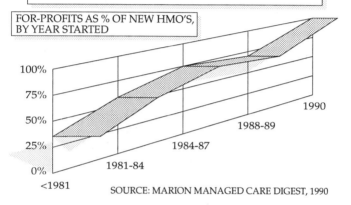

THE RISE OF FOR-PROFIT HMO'S

FOR-PROFITS AS % OF NEW HMO'S, BY YEAR STARTED

100%
75%
50%
25%
0%

<1981
1981-84
1984-87
1988-89
1990

SOURCE: MARION MANAGED CARE DIGEST, 1990

The distinction between HMOs and other kinds of insurance products has blurred. The orginal HMOs were non-profit group practices offering the advantages of an integrated team approach. Most owned their own medical facilities; many had substantial consumer input; and bureaucracy was minimal. In contrast, virtually all new HMOs are owned by for-profit insurance companies, and represent one product line among the many types of insurance that the corporations sell. Most of the new and rapidly growing HMOs own no medical facilities, deliver no clinical care, and have little consumer input. Rather, they represent a new contractual relationship between an insurance company and providers, with the providers increasingly controlled by the insurance company that is the hub of this financial network.

We Could Save $50 Billion/Year in Hospital Costs on the Canadian Plan

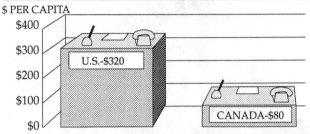

HOSPITAL BILLING AND ADMINISTRATION COSTS UNITED STATES AND CANADA, 1993

$ PER CAPITA

- $400
- $300
- $200
- $100
- $0

U.S.-$320

CANADA-$80

SOURCE: WOOLHANDLER/HIMMELSTEIN NEJM 1991; 324:1253, NEJM 1993; 329:400

Hospital payment is greatly simplified under a single payer system such as Canada's because everyone has the same insurance coverage. Canadian hospitals are paid on a global or lump sum budget basis rather than being paid for each individual service or patient. Since hospitals send almost no bills to individual patients (other than Americans who happen to get sick while visiting Canada) billing departments are tiny. The average U.S. hospital employs about 50 billing personnel; the average Canadian hospital employs 3 or 4.

In Canada, each hospital negotiates its total annual budget with the provincial health insurance program, and receives a single check bi-weekly to cover virtually all costs. There is no need to track which patient got every dose of antibiotics or bottle of IV fluid, allowing the elimination of a great deal of internal cost accounting and expensive computer billing equipment. By 1990, the average U.S. hospital was spending one-quarter of total revenues on billing and administration, compared to roughly 10% in Canada. Overall, the U.S. could save about $50 billion each year on hospital billing by adopting the Canadian global budget-type system.

131

The Billing Bureaucracy

Billing stickers adorn the bodice of this nurses' uniform. She removed the stickers from the supplies needed to insert a central intravenous line in the Intensive Care Unit. Each piece of intravenous tubing and sterile towel has an individually numbered sticker affixed to it in the central supply room. The nurse removes the stickers when the supplies are used, and later places them in the patient's chart. At the end of the hospital stay, the chart is sent to the billing office where several full-time clerk typists enter the billing numbers into a multi-million dollar computer system, and the computer produces the detailed bill which is forwarded to the patient and insurer(s). The insurance company employs a large staff which reviews each item. Finally, patients are liable for any uncovered items, and often spend much of their convalescence dealing with detailed hospital bills.

Clinical Workforce Grows Little While Marketing Mushrooms

PERCENT CHANGE IN HOSPITAL EMPLOYMENT BY OCCUPATION, 1983-1989

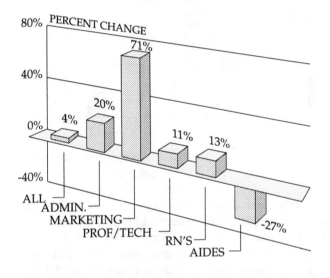

SOURCE: MONTHLY LABOR REVIEW 1991

Most new hospital jobs created over the past decade have been clerical and administrative, while the clinical work force has expanded very little.

U.S. Doctors Spend 2.5 Times More on Billing Expenses than Their Canadian Counterparts

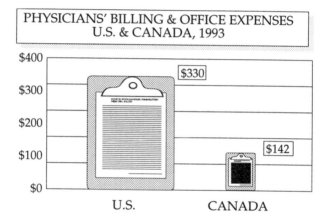

PHYSICIANS' BILLING & OFFICE EXPENSES U.S. & CANADA, 1993

U.S.: $330

CANADA: $142

SOURCE: WOOLHANDLER/HIMMELSTEIN NEJM 1991; 324:1253 - UPDATED 1993

Physicians' billing is far simpler in Canada. Each provincial program has a simple billing form that is used for each patient. The physician or their staff uses the patient's insurance card to stamp the form, checks a single box, and sends all of the forms to the provincial insurance program by mail or computer.

All patients are covered, and bills are paid promptly and in full. There is virtually no utilization review bureaucracy, nor other outside interference in the doctor-patient relationship. As a result, office administration and billing is far less expensive for Canadian physicians than for doctors in the United States.

The U.S. Spends 3 Times More than Canada on Administration

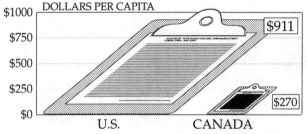

OVERALL ADMINISTRATIVE COSTS
U.S. & CANADA, 1993

DOLLARS PER CAPITA

$911

$270

U.S.   CANADA

SOURCE: WOOLHANDLER/HIMMELSTEIN NEJM 1991; 324:1253- UPDATED 1993

Reducing U.S. administrative costs to the Canadian level would have saved $641 per capita in 1993. These findings were confirmed in a 1991 study by the U.S. General Accounting Office (GAO), the non-partisan investigative agency of the Congress. The GAO estimated that implementing a Canadian-style system in the U.S. would save about 10% of total health spending (more than $90 billion in 1993) by eliminating much of the paperwork and administration of the current U.S. system. Administrative savings would be more than enough to fund comprehensive coverage for all of the uninsured, and to improve the coverage for those who currently have only partial coverage.

The administrative costs included in these calculations fall into 3 categories: insurance overhead and profits; hospital/nursing home administration and billing; and physicians' office administration and billing.

Managers Do Not
Productivity Make

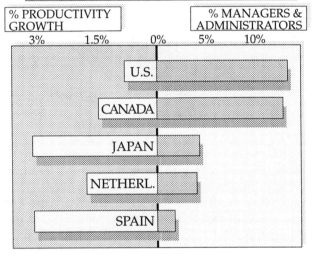

MANAGERS & ADMINISTRATORS
AS % OF WORKERS, 1989
AND PRODUCTIVITY GROWTH, 1979-1990

% PRODUCTIVITY GROWTH

% MANAGERS & ADMINISTRATORS

3%   1.5%   0%   5%   10%

U.S.

CANADA

JAPAN

NETHERL.

SPAIN

SOURCE: ILO YEARBOOK OF LABOR
STATISTICS & OECD ECONOMIC OUTLOOK 50

The U.S. has the most managers per employee of any industrialized nation, yet during the past decade it has had the slowest growth in productivity. Managers are about 6% of the labor force in the average industrialized nation, compared with 12.1% in the U.S. Productivity growth between 1979 and 1990 averaged 2% in the major Western European nations as compared to 0.7% in the United States.

Drug Advertisements Waste Billions

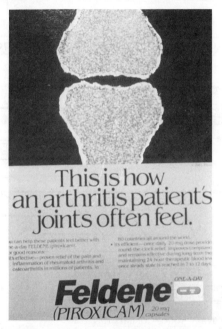

This expensive drug company advertisement appeared in dozens of medical journals in the past decade. The ad includes real sandpaper (a boon for physician woodworkers).

Each year drug firms spend several billion dollars on drug advertising and so-called "detailing," marketing activities intended to influence (and usually worsen) the prescribing habits of American physicians. Promotional activities range from simple advertisements such as that shown in this picture, to outright bribing of physicians with expensive trips and gifts. The costs of such promotions are ultimately borne by patients in the form of higher drug prices.

U.S. Drug Prices 50% Higher than in Canada

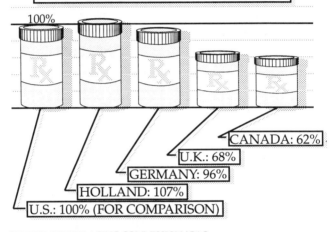

PRESCRIPTION DRUG PRICES
IN FOUR COUNTRIES
COMPARED TO U.S. PRICES

100%

CANADA: 62%

U.K.: 68%

GERMANY: 96%

HOLLAND: 107%

U.S.: 100% (FOR COMPARISON)

SOURCE: SENATE AGING COMMISSION/GAO

Drug companies have faced little pressure to lower prices in the U.S., or in the multiple payer systems of Holland and Germany. Physicians prescribe medications (often with little knowledge of drug costs) and patients pay the bill, but have little influence over what is prescribed. In contrast, under the single payer systems in Canada and the U.K. there is a large and powerful buyer (the government single payer) which has considerable leverage in price negotiations with the drug industry. As a result, Canadians pay only 62% as much as Americans for identical pharmaceuticals.

Medical Malpractice is the Leading Cause of Accidental Death in the U.S.

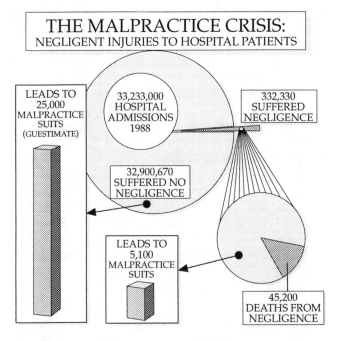

THE MALPRACTICE CRISIS:
NEGLIGENT INJURIES TO HOSPITAL PATIENTS

LEADS TO 25,000 MALPRACTICE SUITS (GUESTIMATE)

33,233,000 HOSPITAL ADMISSIONS 1988

332,330 SUFFERED NEGLIGENCE

32,900,670 SUFFERED NO NEGLIGENCE

LEADS TO 5,100 MALPRACTICE SUITS

45,200 DEATHS FROM NEGLIGENCE

SOURCE: HARVARD MALPRACTICE STUDY, NEJM 1991; 324:370 & 325:245 - NY DATA PROJECTED TO U.S.

The problems in the tort system and the occurrence of frivolous law suits has diverted attention from the great burden of malpractice that patients actually suffer. Medical malpractice is the leading cause of accidental death and injury in the United States, accounting for about 45,000 deaths each year according to the comprehensive study of malpractice in New York State carried out by a Harvard group. Only a tiny proportion, less than 5%, of those who suffer an injury from malpractice actually bring a suit. Unfortunately, many of those who sue are not those who have suffered malpractice. Moreover, about two-thirds of total malpractice insurance premiums end up in the pockets of lawyers and insurance companies.

A national health program could substantially reduce malpractice suits by eliminating the 40% of all claims that seek coverage for future medical care costs. Additional reforms will be necessary to improve the quality of care and reduce the incidence of negligence, as well as to reduce the proportion of malpractice actions that are brought on frivolous grounds.

The claim that tort reform would substantially reduce health care costs is dubious. Malpractice insurance premiums only amount to about 1% of total health spending. Widely circulated estimates of $15-30 billion annually according to the AMA for the costs of "defensive medicine," are based on very poor studies. There is no evidence that costs have risen any less steeply in the several states that have already enacted tort reform.

Spending On the Last Year of Life is *Not* Driving Up Medicare Costs

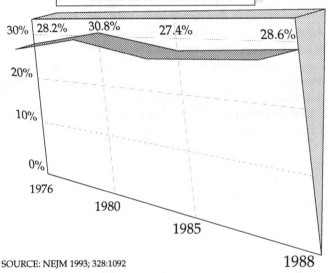

PROPORTION OF MEDICARE SPENDING
IN THE LAST YEAR OF LIFE

28.2%   30.8%   27.4%   28.6%

30%
20%
10%
0%

1976
1980
1985
1988

SOURCE: NEJM 1993; 328:1092

There is a widespread impression that rising health care costs are largely attributable to increasing costs for care of the terminally ill. In fact, less than a third of Medicare spending is devoted to care during the last year of life, and this share has not risen at all since 1976. The proportion of spending for end-of-life care is certainly lower among non-Medicare patients, who are younger and far less likely to die.

Studies clearly show that many patients wish to forego invasive terminal care, but relatively few have discussed this option with their physicians. It seems likely that complying with patients' wishes would save some money. But framing these discussions as a cost containment initiative will poison the atmosphere and sow distrust that doctors are subtly coercing patients and families to accept cheaper care, rather than sharing a decision to die gently.

Aside from grave moral problems attendant on injecting cost considerations into decisions at the end of life, calls to limit the costs of such care ignore the difficulty of divining when the last week or month of life has commenced. Studies of intensive care unit (ICU) patients have found that costs are relatively low for those whose doctors correctly predicted death or recovery at the time of ICU admission. Patients whose deaths or survival are unexpected incur the highest costs.

HIV Is *Not* the Cause of Spiraling Health Costs

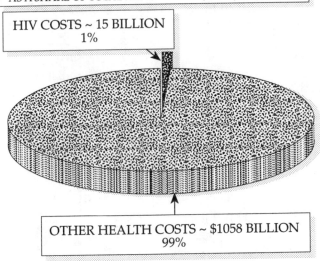

COSTS OF HEALTH CARE FOR PEOPLE WITH HIV
AS A SHARE OF TOTAL HEALTH COSTS, 1995 (PROJECTED)

HIV COSTS ~ 15 BILLION
1%

OTHER HEALTH COSTS ~ $1058 BILLION
99%

SOURCE: HELLINGER - INQUIRY 1992; 29:356 &
HLTH CARE FIN REV 1991; 13(1):1

Care of HIV-related illness is not a major contributor to the increasing costs of medical care. HIV-related health care costs are expected to total $15 billion in 1995, about 1% of total health care costs in that year.

Illegal Drug Abuse Does Not Account for Rising Health Costs

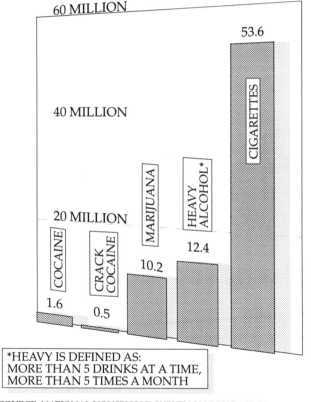

NUMBER OF AMERICANS
ABUSING DRUGS

60 MILLION

53.6

40 MILLION

CIGARETTES

MARIJUANA

HEAVY ALCOHOL*

20 MILLION

COCAINE

CRACK COCAINE

12.4

10.2

1.6

0.5

*HEAVY IS DEFINED AS:
MORE THAN 5 DRINKS AT A TIME,
MORE THAN 5 TIMES A MONTH

SOURCE: NATIONAL HOUSEHOLD SURVEY ON DRUG ABUSE

Tobacco and alcohol abuse are far more prevalent than the abuse of illegal substances.

Abuse of illegal drugs cannot explain high health care costs in the U.S. While estimates of illegal drug-related mortality and morbidity are imprecise, it is clear that tobacco and alcohol cause far more deaths and illnesses than cocaine, heroin or marijuana. According to chart reviews, less than one percent of emergency room (ER) visits involve an illegal drug-related incident. In contrast, alcohol is involved in 18% to 40% of ER episodes. A 1984 report estimated that alcohol was responsible for 59,000 trauma deaths while drugs (including prescription medications) accounted for 21,000. Overall drug-related deaths totaled 30,000 as compared to 98,000 from alcohol and 485,000 from tobacco (Ravenholt. Pop & Dev Rev 1984; 10:697).

Many nations with greater total burdens of substance abuse (alcohol + tobacco + illegal drugs) have far lower health costs than the U.S. For instance, Canada's drinking and smoking rates were higher than ours until the late 1980s when a huge increase in cigarette taxes precipitously lowered Canada's tobacco consumption.

SYLVIA

by Nicole Hollander

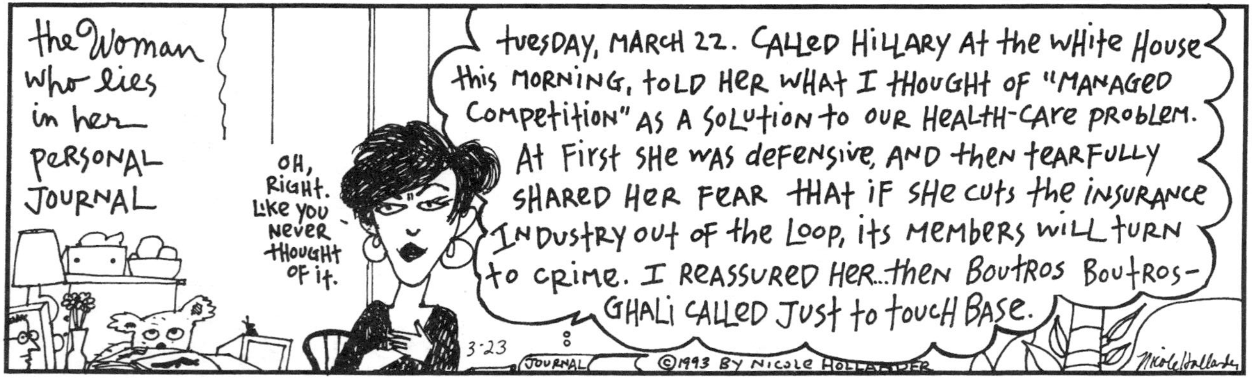

Part VII

A National Health Program for the U.S.

A Canadian-style national health program (NHP) for the United States would cover everyone but cost no more than we currently spend. A single payer insurance system could eliminate $100 billion now wasted each year on bureaucracy. Additional billions could be saved by removing incentives for unnecessary tests, operations, and the expensive duplication of facilities. New taxes to fund the national health program would replace insurance premiums and out-of-pocket medical expenses. Initially, costs for the average American would be no higher under the NHP than under the current system. In the long run, the NHP would effectively contain costs and save tens of billions.

Essentials of a
National Health Program

▶ UNIVERSAL, COMPREHENSIVE
COVERAGE

▶ NO OUT-OF-POCKET PAYMENTS

▶ HOSPITALS PAID "LUMP SUM"
OPERATING BUDGETS

▶ SEPARATE CAPITAL BUDGETS

▶ A SINGLE, PUBLIC PAYER

▶ PUBLIC ACCOUNTABILITY BUT
MINIMAL BUREAUCRACY

SOURCE: HIMMELSTEIN, WOOLHANDLER NEJM 1989; 320:102

1-Everyone must be covered under a single comprehensive program to eliminate two class care, assure universal access, and realize the administrative savings that are only possible under a single payer system.

2-All out-of-pocket payments for medically necessary services must be eliminated.

3-Hospitals must be paid lump sum global operating budgets rather than billing on a per patient basis. This allows the virtual abolition of hospital billing and most internal cost accounting.

4-Capital budgets must be separated from operating budgets. The separate appropriation of capital funds would facilitate rational health planning, and discourage hospitals from skimping on care in order to accumulate funds for expansion.

5-A single public payer must administer the system. The single payer is the *sine qua non* of administrative simplification. Public administration is far more efficient than administration by private insurers. Private insurance overhead averages more than 13%, while Canada's public program runs for less than 1% (0.7%) overhead, and the Medicare program in the U.S. has an overhead of about 3%.

6-Public accountability is vital, but should not be accomplished through bureaucratic intrusion in the details of clinical practice. A single payer system allows the monitoring of patterns of practice, with more detailed reviews reserved for physicians displaying outlandish practice patterns. The case-by-case oversight characteristic of current utilization review methods should be minimized, as in Canada and in other nations with single payer systems.

149

The NHP Would Eliminate Financial Barriers to Access

COVERAGE UNDER THE NATIONAL HEALTH PROGRAM

▶ UNIVERSAL ~ EVERYONE COVERED

▶ COMPREHENSIVE ~ ALL MEDICALLY NECESSARY CARE (INCLUDING LONG TERM CARE), NO OUT-OF-POCKET COSTS

▶ A SINGLE, PUBLICLY ADMINISTERED PLAN ~ CURTAILS BUREAUCRACY, AIDS COST CONTROL

▶ ELIMINATE COMPETING PRIVATE INSURANCE ~ FACILITATES COST CONTROL, DISCOURAGES TWO CLASS CARE

SOURCE: HIMMELSTEIN, WOOLHANDLER NEJM 1989; 320:102

Universal coverage would solve the gravest problem in health care by eliminating financial barriers to access. A single comprehensive program is necessary both to insure equal access to care and to minimize the complexity and expense of billing and administration. Public administration of insurance funds would save tens of billions of dollars each year. The more than 1,200 private health insurers in the U.S. now consume about 13% of revenues for overhead, whereas the Medicare program and Canada's national health program have overhead costs of 3% and 0.7% respectively. Failure to ban competing private insurance would require the continuation of the costly bureaucracies that administer and deal with such programs, and would continually endanger the adequacy of funding for the public program. Private insurance would only be attractive if the public coverage were inadequate, assuring insurance industry lobbying to undermine the public program. Allowing wealthy Americans to buy out of the public system would erode the support of this powerful group for adequate public funding of the national health program.

Co-payments and deductibles endanger the health of poor people who are sick, decrease the use of vital inpatient medical services as much as the use of unnecessary ones, discourage preventive care, and are unwieldy and expensive to administer. Moreover, experience in Canada and other nations demonstrates that co-payments and deductibles do not lower overall costs because doctors, not patients largely determine the volume of services. The Canadian data demonstrate that co-payments decrease utilization by the poor, but physicians compensate by scheduling more frequent visits by wealthier patients and keep their calendars full. Hence, co-payments and deductibles do not lower overall costs. This system-wide effect cannot be demonstrated by studies, such as the Rand Health Insurance Experiment in the United States, in which a relatively small number of patients in a community are assigned increased co-payments and observed. In these studies, only a very small proportion of any one physician's practice is affected. Hence the compensatory increase in utilization by more affluent patients is very small, and mostly experienced by people not enrolled in the study.

Paying for Physicians Under the National Health Program

I. *Fee for service* with mandatory assignment and simplified, negotiated fee schedule.

II. *Capitation* for institutions employing salaried physicians. Free disenrollment required, selective enrollment prohibited. Capitation fee covers operating costs only, may not be used for capital purchases, profits, or physician incentives. Inpatient care covered under hospital global budgets.

III. *Global Budgeted Institutions* (eg. hospitals, clinics, home care agencies) with salaried physicians.

SOURCE: WOOLHANDLER/HIMMELSTEIN NEJM 1989; 320:102

To minimize the disruption of existing patterns of care, the NHP would include three payment options for physicians and other practitioners: fee-for-service, salaries from institutions receiving global budgets, and salaries from group practices or HMOs receiving capitation payments.

Fee-for-service payments would be based on a negotiated, simplified, binding fee schedule. Physicians would submit bills to the NHP on a simple form or by computer and would receive extra payment for any bill not paid within 30 days. Physicians who accepted payment from the NHP could bill patients directly only for uncovered services (e.g., purely cosmetic surgery). Payments to physicians or HMOs would not cover capital costs, which would be reimbursed from the separate capital budget (as in the case of hospitals).

This simplified payment and billing mechanism would eliminate a great deal of paperwork for physicians, and greatly streamline bureaucracy. The average physician's office overhead expense would be reduced by between $20,000 and $30,000 per year.

Capital Payment Can Be Planned to Meet Costs Effectively

CAPITAL PAYMENT
AND
PLANNING
UNDER A
NATIONAL HEALTH PLAN

 Operating Budgets cannot be diverted to capital

 All funds distributed by NHP Health Planning Boards

 No privately funded capital that increases operating expenses

SOURCE: WOOLHANDLER/HIMMELSTEIN NEJM 1989; 320:102

Current capital spending determines future operating costs, as well as the distribution of facilities. Under the existing payment system, which combines operating and capital payments, prosperous hospitals and HMOs can expand and modernize, whereas impoverished ones cannot, regardless of the health needs of their patient populations or the quality of services they provide. The NHP would replace this implicit mechanism for distributing capital with an explicit one, facilitating (though not guaranteeing) allocation on the basis of need and quality. In order to achieve these goals, the NHP would prohibit providers from diverting operating funds to the purchase or lease of capital. All capital funds would be distributed by the national health program's planning boards. Capital projects funded by private donations would require approval by the health planning board if they entailed an increase in future operating expenses.

Prohibiting the use of operating funds for capital purchases or profits would eliminate the main financial incentive for both excessive intervention (under fee-for-service payment) and skimping on care (under DRG-type prospective payment systems), since neither inflating revenues nor limiting care could profit the institution. The separate appropriation of capital funds would facilitate rational health planning. This method of hospital payment has successfully contained costs, minimized bureaucracy, improved the distribution of health resources, and maintained quality of care in Canada and several western European nations.

Hospitals Can Be Successfully Operated with the NHP

HOSPITAL PAYMENT
UNDER A
NATIONAL HEALTH PROGRAM

 Hospitals remain Privately Owned and Run.

 Negotiated Global Budget for all Operating Costs. Operating Funds cannot be diverted to Capital

 Capital Purchases/Expansion budgeted seperately based on health planning goals

SOURCE: WOOLHANDLER/HIMMELSTEIN NEJM 1989; 320:102

The NHP would pay each hospital an annual lump-sum to cover all operating expenses. The state's NHP payment board and the hospital would negotiate the amount of this payment based on past expenditures, previous financial and clinical performance, projected changes in levels of services, wages and other costs, and proposed new and innovative programs. Hospitals would not bill for services covered by the NHP. No part of the operating budget could be used for hospital expansion, profit, marketing, or major capital purchases or leases. These expenditures would also come from the NHP fund, but they would be financed through separate appropriations.

Global budgeting of hospitals would save more than half of total hospital administrative costs, equivalent to about 15% of total hospital costs. This would free up substantial resources for increased clinical care.

A Health Plan
to Cover Everyone

PATIENT'S VIEW OF A
NATIONAL HEALTH PROGRAM

▶ UNIVERSAL ACCESS TO COMPREHENSIVE CARE

▶ NO OUT-OF-POCKET COSTS

▶ COMPLETE FREE CHOICE OF DOCTOR & HOSPITAL

▶ NO INSURANCE HASSLES

SOURCE: HIMMELSTEIN, WOOLHANDLER NEJM 1989; 320:102

The national health program would establish a right to comprehensive care. As in Canada, each person would receive a national health program card entitling him or her to all necessary medical care without co-payments of deductibles. This card could be used with any practitioner and at any institution. Thus, the NHP would give patients a free choice of providers and eliminate the financial threat of illness. Taxes would increase by an amount equivalent to the current total of medical expenditures by individuals. Conversely, individuals' payments for medical care would decrease by the same amount. In the first few years of the NHP the average American would see little change in their current overall health costs. Over the longer run, the slowed rate of health care cost increases under an NHP would result in lower costs.

Providing Care
for the Disabled in the Community

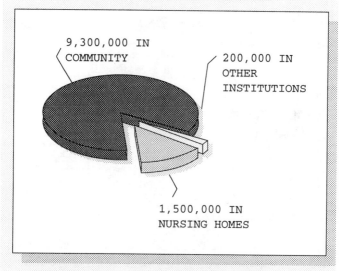

WHERE THE DISABLED LIVE

9,300,000 IN COMMUNITY

200,000 IN OTHER INSTITUTIONS

1,500,000 IN NURSING HOMES

SOURCE: NATIONAL CENTER FOR HEALTH STATISTICS
AND AMERICAN HOSPITAL ASSOCIATION

About 85% of those with disabilities live in the community, while only about 15% are in nursing homes or other institutions. Hence, any long term care program must assure substantial attention to providing care for those with disabilities living in the community.

Few Have Private Insurance For Long-Term Care

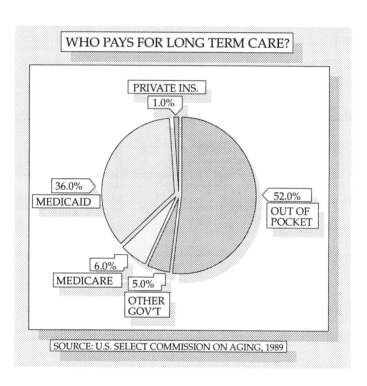

WHO PAYS FOR LONG TERM CARE?

PRIVATE INS.
1.0%

36.0%
MEDICAID

52.0%
OUT OF
POCKET

6.0%
MEDICARE

5.0%

OTHER
GOV'T

SOURCE: U.S. SELECT COMMISSION ON AGING, 1989

At present most long-term care costs are borne directly by patients and their families. Medicaid pays for most of the rest. Private insurance pays only 1% of long-term care costs. No more than 40%, and perhaps as few as 6% of the elderly could afford adequate private long-term care insurance policies.

Long-Term Care
Given by Families and Friends
Must be Valued and Supported

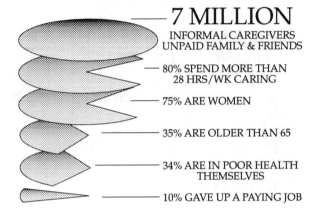

— 7 MILLION
INFORMAL CAREGIVERS
UNPAID FAMILY & FRIENDS

— 80% SPEND MORE THAN
28 HRS/WK CARING

— 75% ARE WOMEN

— 35% ARE OLDER THAN 65

— 34% ARE IN POOR HEALTH
THEMSELVES

— 10% GAVE UP A PAYING JOB

More than 70% of those receiving long-term care (3.2 million people) rely exclusively on informal (unpaid) care givers. About 22% use both formal and informal care, while 5% use only formal care.

Of the more than seven million informal care givers, 75% are women, 35% are themselves over 65 years old, 33% are in poor health, 10% have given up paid employment to assume the care of their loved one, and 8 of 10 spend at least 4 hours every day providing care. Such personal devotion can never be replaced by the assistance of even the kindest of strangers. It must be valued and supported rather than supplanted by formal care.

Goals for Long-Term Care

▶ A UNIVERSAL RIGHT TO LONG TERM CARE

▶ CONSUMER CHOICE

▶ INDEPENDENT LIVING

▶ QUALITY

▶ COORDINATE WITH ACUTE CARE

▶ SPREAD FINANCIAL RISK

▶ SUPPORT INFORMAL CAREGIVERS

SOURCE: JAMA 1991; 266:3023

1-Long-term care should be a right of all Americans, not a commodity available only to the wealthy and the destitute.

2-Coverage should be universal, with access to services based on need rather than age, cause of disability, or income.

3-Long-term care should provide a continuum of social and medical services aimed at maximizing functional independence.

4-Medically and socially oriented long-term care should be coordinated with acute care.

5-The program should encourage accessible, efficient, and innovative systems of delivery.

6-The program should promote high quality services and appropriate utilization in the least restrictive environment possible.

7-A progressive financing system should spread the financial risk across the entire population. The misfortune of disability should not be compounded by the specter of financial ruin.

8-The importance of informal care should be acknowledged. Support, financial and other, should be offered to assist, rather than supplant, home and community care givers.

9-Consumers should have a range of choices and culturally appropriate options for long-term care.

The Meaning of Comprehensive Care

LONG TERM CARE
UNDER THE
NATIONAL HEALTH PROGRAM

- A UNIFORM PACKAGE OF SOCIAL AND MEDICAL SERVICES.

- INSTITUTIONAL CARE: INDEPENDENT LIVING CENTERS, REHABILITATION & STATE HOSPITALS,NURSING HOMES.

- COMMUNITY-BASED CARE: ASSESSMENT, BOARD AND CARE, HOME HEALTH AND ADULT DAY CARE.

- HOME CARE: MEALS, HOMEMAKERS, TRANSPORTATION, HOME HEALTH.

- SUPPORT FOR INFORMAL CAREGIVERS: TRAINING, SUPPORT GROUPS, RESPITE CARE, OCCASIONALLY COMPENSATION.

SOURCE: JAMA 1991; 266:3023

Everyone would be covered for all medically and socially necessary services under a single public plan. Home and community-based benefits would include nursing, therapy services, case management, meals, information and referrals, in-home support (homemaker and attendant) services, respite, transportation, adult day care, social day care, psychiatric day care, hospice, community mental health, and other related services. Residential services would include foster care, board and care, assisted living, and residential care facilities. Institutional care would include nursing homes, chronic care hospitals, and rehabilitation facilities. Drug and alcohol treatment, outpatient rehabilitation, and independent living programs would also be covered. In special circumstances, other services might be covered such as supported employment and training, financial management, legal services, protective services, senior companions, and payment for informal care givers. Acute care services would also be covered, as outlined elsewhere.

A long-term care (LTC) payment board in each state would contract directly with providers through a network of local public agencies responsible for eligibility determination and care coordination. Nursing homes, home care agencies and other institutional providers would be paid a global budget. HMOs and other integrated provider organizations could receive a capitation fee to cover LTC and acute care services. Individual practitioners could continue to be paid on a fee-for-service basis, or could receive salaries from institutional providers. For-profit providers would be compensated for past investment and phased out.

Comprehensive coverage permits use of the most appropriate services and may prevent unnecessary hospitalization or institutional placement. Since most individuals needing LTC prefer to remain at home, services should promote independent living and support informal care givers, using nursing homes as the last resort rather than as the primary approach to LTC. Services must be culturally appropriate for special population groups including ethnic, cultural, and religious minorities; the oldest old; individuals who are mentally impaired or developmentally disabled; children; and young adults.

The Quality of Long-Term Care Must Be Improved

- UNIFORM NATIONAL STANDARDS FOR: STRUCTURE, PROCESS & OUTCOME.

- QA PROGRAMS AT ALL INSTITUTIONS.

- CONSOLIDATE REGULATION.

- TRAINING AND WAGE INCREASES FOR LTC WORKERS.

- RESEARCH ON QA FOR LTC.

- CONSUMER CHOICE.

SOURCE: JAMA 1991; 266:3023

No other segment of the health care system has as many documented quality problems as the nursing home industry and concern is growing about the quality of home care. As many as one-third of all nursing homes currently operate below the minimal federal standards. Monitoring the quality of LTC has been hindered by variability in state regulatory programs and a lack of well-validated standards and procedures.

The NHP would require each LTC provider to meet uniform national quality standards. These standards would include structural measures (e.g., staffing levels, educational requirements), process measures (e.g., individualized planning and provision of care), and outcome measures (e.g., changes in functional or mental status, incontinence, mortality rates, and hospital admission rates). Earmarked funds from the federal LTC budget would support research to validate and improve standards and to develop new approaches to quality assurance (QA).

Each LTC organization would be required to establish a QA program and a quality review committee with representatives of each category of service provider as well as clients and their families.

Funding would also be allocated for improving the wages and training of LTC workers. At present LTC workers earn 15% to 45% less than comparable hospital employees, and many LTC workers are sorely undertrained.

Part VIII

A Plan to Afford a National Health Program:

- Paying in Taxes What We Now Pay in Premiums;
- Covering Everyone at No Additional Cost

Getting
From Here to There

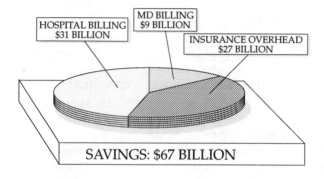

SAVINGS AND NEW COSTS UNDER THE
NATIONAL HEALTH PROGRAM
(1991 DOLLARS)

MD BILLING
$9 BILLION

HOSPITAL BILLING
$31 BILLION

INSURANCE OVERHEAD
$27 BILLION

SAVINGS: $67 BILLION

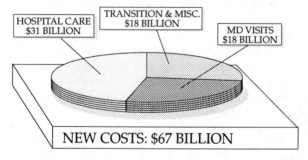

HOSPITAL CARE
$31 BILLION

TRANSITION & MISC.
$18 BILLION

MD VISITS
$18 BILLION

NEW COSTS: $67 BILLION

As described in the May 15, 1991 *Journal of the American Medical Association,* Physicians for a National Health Program has developed a transition budget for the NHP. All figures are given in 1991 dollars.

Hospitals could eliminate most billing and internal cost accounting, saving $31 billion on hospital bureaucracy in the first year. Hospital budgets would not be reduced to reflect these savings, but would be left at current levels. The resources freed up by curtailing bureaucracy would be available to increase clinical care and meet the expected demand surge. For instance, billing personnel could be transferred to clinical departments to perform clerical duties, freeing up nurses for bedside care.

Similarly, though physicians would save about $9 billion on decreased billing and paperwork costs, total payments to physicians would actually increase by $9 billion over current physician expenditures to reflect the expected higher rates of utilization under the NHP.

Another $18 billion would be budgeted for the expansion of long-term care, job training and placement programs for displaced administrative workers, and other transition costs. Overall, we estimate that implementing an NHP would be budget neutral—the administrative savings would cover the costs of increased demand for care. This estimate has been confirmed by the U.S. General Accounting Office, the non-partisan investigative office of the Congress, which has estimated that a Canadian-style NHP could actually save $3 billion in health spending while extending universal access. The Congressional Budget Office has produced a similar estimate.

Savings in Efficiency Would Provide Better Coverage for All

COSTS: NHP VS. CURRENT POLICIES

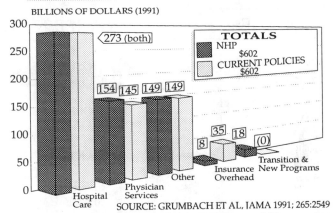

BILLIONS OF DOLLARS (1991)

TOTALS
NHP $602
CURRENT POLICIES $602

273 (both) — Hospital Care
154 145 — Physician Services
149 149 — Other
8 35 — Insurance Overhead
18 (0) — Transition & New Programs

SOURCE: GRUMBACH ET AL, JAMA 1991; 265:2549

Initially, total costs under the NHP would be equivalent to health costs in the current system. Improved coverage for the uninsured as well as for the tens of millions of Americans with only partial coverage would be funded by administrative savings achieved through the efficiency of a single payer system.

Overall expenditures for hospital care would remain the same. However, hospitals would be relieved of substantial administrative burdens and could transfer billing personnel and administrative resources into clinical care to meet the expected surge in demand. An additional $9 billion would be available for physician services to meet the expected substantial increase in demand. Insurance overhead would be cut by at least $27 billion, reflecting the far greater efficiency of a single payer. The $18 billion derived from these administrative savings would be available for the expansion of long-term care, retraining and placement of displaced administrative workers, and other transition costs.

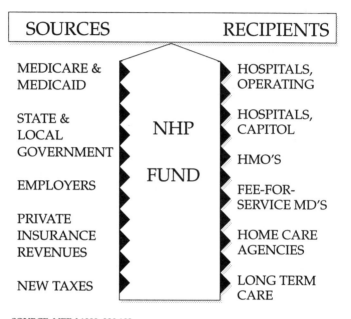

Average Americans Would Pay No Extra: Taxes Would Replace Premiums and Out-of-Pocket Costs

SOURCES	RECIPIENTS
MEDICARE & MEDICAID	HOSPITALS, OPERATING
STATE & LOCAL GOVERNMENT	HOSPITALS, CAPITOL
	HMO'S
EMPLOYERS	FEE-FOR-SERVICE MD'S
PRIVATE INSURANCE REVENUES	HOME CARE AGENCIES
NEW TAXES	LONG TERM CARE

NHP FUND

SOURCE: NEJM 1989; 320:102

The NHP would disburse virtually all payments for health services. The total expenditure would be set at the same proportion of the Gross National Product as health costs represented in the year preceding the implementation of the NHP. Funds could be raised through a variety of mechanisms, though funding based on a graduated income tax or other progressive tax would be the fairest. Tax-based funding is the least cumbersome and least expensive mechanism for collecting money.

During the transition, funding that mimicked existing patterns would minimize economic disruption. All current federal funds allocated to Medicare and Medicaid would be paid to the NHP, as would all current state and local expenditures for health care. A tax earmarked for the NHP would be levied on all employers, with the tax rate set so that total collections equalled the previous year's total of employer's expenditures for health benefits, adjusted for inflation. Additional taxes equivalent to the amount now spent by individuals for insurance premiums and out-of-pocket costs would be levied.

It is critical that all funds for health care flow through the NHP. Such single-source payment has been the cornerstone of cost containment and administrative efficiency in Canada. Overall, average American would pay no more for health care under the NHP than they do at present. However, rather than paying insurance premiums, co-payments, deductibles, property taxes used to fund health benefits for municipal employees, etc., they would pay health care taxes.

Expand Long-Term Care to Meet Need

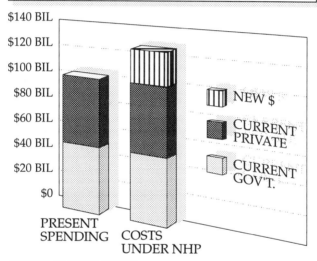

FUNDING FOR LONG-TERM CARE
NOW AND UNDER NHP

SOURCE: JAMA 1991; 266:3023

We propose expanding funding for LTC by between $18 and $23.5 billion over current levels of expenditures. This would allow a 20% increase in nursing home utilization and more than a 50% increase in home health care, as well as substantial pay increases for long-term care workers. (All figures are given in 1990 dollars.)

Quality Long-Term Care Is Affordable

TAX OPTIONS FOR LONG TERM CARE AND REVENUE GENERATED

- 1% PAYROLL TAX ON WORKERS AND EMPLOYERS

    $50 BILLION

- INCREASE INCOME TAX 7%

    $30 BILLION

- 5% CORPORATE INCOME SURTAX

    $6 BILLION

- REMOVE SOCIAL SECURITY EARNINGS CAP

    $49 BILLION

- 10% SURTAX ON ESTATES > $200,000

    $4 BILLION

- TAX CAPITAL GAINS AT DEATH

    $6 BILLION

SOURCE: BALL RM & BETHELL TN, 1989

A number of potential tax options that could generate additional revenues for the support of long-term care. Note that **only a few of these options would be needed to fund the NHP.**

Today, the Poor Pay the Most

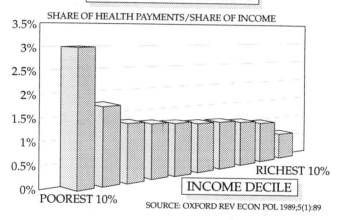

THE REGRESSIVITY OF
U.S.HEALTH FINANCING

SHARE OF HEALTH PAYMENTS/SHARE OF INCOME

RICHEST 10%

INCOME DECILE

POOREST 10%

SOURCE: OXFORD REV ECON POL 1989;5(1):89

This chart displays the pattern of overall health financing under the current U.S. system. The poorest 10% of the population pays approximately 6 times more, as a proportion of their income, for health care than the wealthiest 10%.

The 10% of the population with the lowest incomes is shown on the far left, and the highest earning 10% on the far right. The intervening bars represent the other 8 income deciles. The height of each bar indicates the proportion of income devoted to health spending for persons in that income decile (relative to the society-wide average).

The Clinton Plan:
The Poor Would *Still* Pay the Most

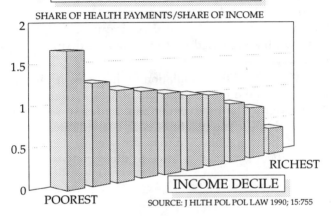

WHO PAYS FOR
EMPLOYER-BASED COVERAGE

SHARE OF HEALTH PAYMENTS/SHARE OF INCOME

INCOME DECILE

POOREST

RICHEST

SOURCE: J HLTH POL POL LAW 1990; 15:755

This chart displays the current distribution of costs for employer-based coverage by income groups within the U.S. Most economists agree that employer-provided benefits are, in effect, deductions from employee wages. Health benefit costs are generally equivalent for the highest paid and for the lowest paid worker in a firm. Hence, the $4,000 cost of a typical health insurance policy is deducted from the $15,000 wages of a lower paid worker, and the same $4,000 deduction applies to a million-dollar-a-year CEO. As a result, the richer an individual, the lower the proportion of income devoted to employer-based insurance.

Employer mandate proposals for reforming health

care (such as President Clinton's plan) might actually increase the overall regressiveness of health financing. Under these programs the uninsured, many of whom currently receive considerable amounts of free care, would be covered by employer paid coverage, the cost of which would ultimately reduce the employee's wages. Economic modeling suggests that the value of the increased care provided to these individuals would be less than the increased cost of insurance deducted from their wages.

The 10% of the population with the lowest incomes is shown on the far left, and the highest earning 10% on the far right. The intervening bars represent the other 8 income deciles. The height of each bar indicates the proportion of income devoted to health spending for persons in that income decile (relative to the society-wide average).

Who Would Pay with a Progressive Tax

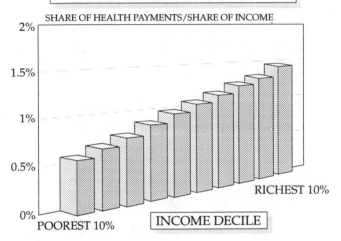

SHARE OF HEALTH PAYMENTS
WITH A PROGRESSIVE INCOME TAX

SHARE OF HEALTH PAYMENTS/SHARE OF INCOME

RICHEST 10%

POOREST 10%   INCOME DECILE

This chart illustrates the concept of funding health care through a progressive tax. The higher an individual's income, the greater would be the proportion of income taken in taxes to pay for care.

The 10% of the population with the lowest incomes is shown on the far left, and the highest earning 10% on the far right. The intervening bars represent the other 8 income deciles. The height of each bar indicates the proportion of income devoted to health spending for persons in that income decile (relative to the society-wide average).

Payment for Canada's NHP is Progressive

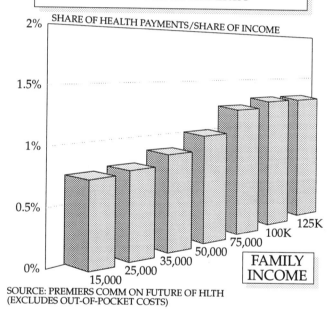

WHO PAYS FOR CANADA'S NHP?
PROVINCE OF ALBERTA

SHARE OF HEALTH PAYMENTS/SHARE OF INCOME

FAMILY INCOME

SOURCE: PREMIERS COMM ON FUTURE OF HLTH
(EXCLUDES OUT-OF-POCKET COSTS)

This chart displays the actual pattern of funding of the health plan in the Canadian province of Alberta. Because the program is funded through progressive taxes, wealthier individuals devote a greater a proportion of their income to health costs than do the poor.

TAXES + PRIVATE HEALTH PAYMENTS COMBINED
ARE EQUIVALENT IN CANADA AND THE U.S.

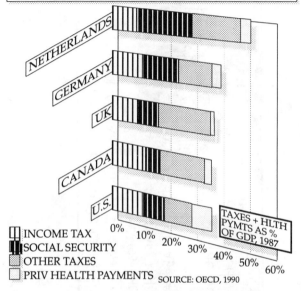

SOURCE: OECD, 1990

The U.S. has the lowest tax burden of any major industrialized nation. However, contrary to widespread perception, Canada's taxes are only slightly higher. The perception of a high tax burden in Canada is fueled by her higher income and sales taxes. However, Canadian social security and real estate taxes are lower than in the U.S.

When private health payments are added to the tax burden, the Canadian and U.S. figures are almost identical. About 37% of total gross domestic product (the value of all goods and services produced within a nation) goes for taxes and private health payments in the two nations.

Part IX

President Clinton's Plan: Making Insurance Companies the Feudal Lords of American Medicine

Stripped of rhetoric, Managed Competition is a plan to push all but the wealthy into a few cut rate HMOs, owned by insurance giants such as Prudential. Since only the wealthy could afford higher cost plans, Managed Competition would ratify a system of care stratified along class lines, separate and unequal.

HMOs have been shown to do poorly at containing costs. Across the the United States, a higher market share commanded by HMOs correlates with higher health costs.

The Clinton Health Plan: A Grimm Fairytale

It took eight months, but the president's health care task force got the details right: measures to encourage primary care training and the development of rural health care resources; a tobacco tax; a nod to the special needs of inner cities; elaborate regulation of insurers; and of course, the finely-honed rhetoric of choice, security, and simplicity. Unfortunately, these details embellish a fundamentally disastrous plan, unable to deliver on its promises but sure to complete the corporate transformation of American medicine. Seeking health reform middle ground between competition and regulation, President Clinton has melded the worst of both. He would:

- Rely on market forces to hold down costs, pushing ahead with a doctrine that has guided federal policy through 20 years of failure, and spawned myriad unsuccessful state and private sector cost control initiatives.

- Assure a multi-tiered health care system by pushing all but the wealthy into stripped down versions of HMOs, run by insurance companies more interested in profit than quality.

- Deny most patients the right to choose or change their doctor and hospital, completing the transformation of American medicine from one-on-one doctor-patient relationships to a medical system run by insurance giants like Prudential and Aetna.

- Ship nearly $300 billion in new business to the

insurance companies who have caused the current crisis, a move sure to raise bureaucratic costs.

- Call on low and middle income families to shoulder most costs.

- Install a huge new regulatory apparatus to oversee costs for employers and government (but leave individuals unprotected). This Frankenstein version of the simple Canadian budgeting mechanisms won't cut costs or assure quality, but will increase bureaucracy.

Clinton's plan cannot contain costs and is hence unlikely to extend coverage. Even before its official release, White House lieutenants spoke of delaying the phase-in of universal coverage to soften the cost impact. Predictably, discussion will turn from mandated coverage to tax incentives and targets. Five years after the passage of Dukakis' universal health insurance law, Massachusetts has more, not fewer uninsured. As costs have soared, the phase-in of the employer mandate has been postponed, then aborted. Like Dukakis, Clinton designed and timed his legislation to boost his (re)election prospects by coupling undeliverable promises of eventual access with immediate payoffs to the mightiest of the powers that be.

The president's evanescent pledge of broader coverage distracts attention from outcomes that his plan can guarantee: entrenched bureaucracy, and obliteration of the last vestiges of non-corporate care. A handful of insurance companies will own or control the entire health care system, its hospitals, clinics and laboratories, and employ nearly all physicians; a single payer reform will be all the more difficult.

Managed Competition: Prudential's Choice

"For [Prudential] the best-case scenario for reform—preferable even to the status quo—would be enactment of a managed competition proposal."

—Bill Link, Executive V.P.,
Prudential

Most of the president's plan adheres to the complex Managed Competition model developed by the Jackson Hole Group with the financial backing of the big insurers. The "short" version of his plan runs to 245 pages, impenetrable to anyone lacking a Ph.D. in health policy (see accompanying summary). This opacity obscures the central theme—find a way to keep insurance giants at the heart of health care. Indeed, while the president loudly declaims against the Health Insurance Association of America (HIAA—the trade association of the smaller insurers) and other "special interests" who oppose his plan, the biggest insurers—Aetna, Prudential, Cigna, Metropolitan Life, Travelers, Blue Cross—all support his approach, along with the American Hospital Association.

Managed Competition theory ascribes the soaring cost of health care to overinsurance and a lack of competition in the medical marketplace. Americans, too insulated from the costs of care, are choosing to be profligate health care consumers. Hence they must be forced to be more cost conscious (by receiving only a low, fixed-employer contribution towards coverage, with employees paying the full extra cost for anything more than a bare bones plan), and aided (through "Health Alliances") in bargaining with insurers to augment competition.

The powerful Health Alliances would lean on the insurance companies/HMOs to lower premiums. They, in turn, would discipline doctors and hospitals by denying contracts to any who refused to comply with insurance company cost-cutting directives. Since only a few managed care plans, giants like Aetna and Prudential, would have the financial clout to assemble the extensive networks needed to compete, they would enroll virtually all patients in a region. Doctors and hospitals denied contracts would be forced out of business/practice, as would smaller insurers and small HMOs. (Hence the HIAA's opposition).

Managed Competition has never worked anywhere. Its proponents' belief in overinsurance remains unshaken by data showing that Americans pay the world's highest out-of-pocket costs, while receiving fewer doctor visits, hospital days, and even transplants than people in Canada and several other nations with much lower health care costs.

The Competition Mirage

Faith in medical competition is similarly ill-founded. Clinton's pro-managed care, pro-competition strategy represents merely an intensification of government and corporate policies that commenced with Richard Nixon's HMO act of 1973. Indeed, Paul Ellwood, convener of the Jackson Hole Group that spearheaded Managed Competition, coined the term "HMO" in the early 1970s, and personally sold Nixon on the concept as a counter to Ted Kennedy's single payer national health insurance proposal. Despite 20 years of failure, Managed Competition advocates see light at the tunnel's end, and urge us to press on.

The rapid expansion of HMOs in the past two decades (about 40 million people are now enrolled in HMOs and more than half of all employees are covered by some form of managed care) has coincided with unprecedented cost increases. One-third of all Californians are enrolled in HMOs, and more than 80% of all employees are covered by some form of managed care. Yet costs there are 19% above the national average and rising more rapidly. Massachusetts and Minnesota, the second and third highest HMO penetration states, have similarly undistinguished cost records. Nationwide, premiums for HMOs are rising at virtually the same rate as traditional Blue Cross and other indemnity insurers' premiums.

Over the past decade a growing number of big employers and state Medicaid programs have engaged in the kind of hard bargaining envisioned for the Health Alliances, with no noticeable effect on health care costs. The Federal Employee Health Benefits Program (FEHBP), touted by many as a model for Managed Competition, has averaged double-digit rate increases since 1984; its costs rose faster in the 1980's than overall health care costs. Furthermore, because the FEHBP (like Clinton's proposal) fixes the employer's contribution and requires employees to bear the full extra cost of better plans, the predictable multi-tiered system has emerged; higher income workers have better health plans. Similarly, the California Public Employees' Retirement System (CALPERS), Clinton's exemplar of Managed Competition, had cost increases exceeding the national average for three of the last five years. Moreover, CALPERS' lower premium increases in the past two years may just mean that costs were shifted to employees via higher out-of-pocket costs, or to non-CALPERS insurance purchasers.

Managed Competition would be further undermined by insurers' efforts to compete by gaming the system rather than by real cost savings. Since 10% of the popula-

The Clinton Health Plan: A Grimm Fairytale

tion consumes 72% of health care, the easiest way for insurers/HMOs to undercut their competitors' prices is to quietly avoid enrolling sick people in the first place, and drive away the chronically ill by offering unsatisfactory care. Immense financial reward accrues to insurers that successfully avoid risk, assuring extraordinary creativity in circumventing Clinton's complex regulatory bans on risk selection. In Medicare's HMO Demonstration Project, regulatory oversight failed to avert even flagrant abuses.

Similarly, Clinton's arcane regulatory structure would introduce myriad new ways to game the system, such as "capitation creep." Health Alliances would no doubt pay plans a higher capitation fee for diabetics. Clever insurance company MBAs would quickly recommend screening glucose tolerance test for all enrollees (preferably immediately after a large lunch), affixing the dubious label "diabetic" to millions. Complex reimbursement and regulatory systems are easier, not harder, to circumvent. The plan is a lobbyist's dream. Removing almost any sentence from the 245 page document would open loopholes worth billions.

The president's plan would wipe out small insurers, leaving a few giant managed care plans, and little competition. Already, ten insurers control 70% of the HMO market nationwide. Only the largest plans have the financial resources to assemble the nationwide networks necessary for contracts with big employers like GM, or even the region-wide networks required for Health Alliance contracts. Big plans also have the war chests needed to game the system through marketing, subtle risk selection and capitation creep (Prudential has already hired William Roper, former head of HCFA and the CDC, to run its health policy/epidemiology unit). They also have clout to extract discounts from hospitals and doctors by threatening to withdraw a large chunk of business. The result: costs shifted to smaller plans, driving up their premiums, and driving away their subscribers. Having muscled out their competitors, the remaining plans will enjoy a quasi-monopoly, foreclosing price competition. As *The New Yorker* put it: "When the Big Three ran the auto industry, they controlled prices very effectively, and no one imagines that compact health care plans from Japan will ever penetrate (or even be allowed to enter) this market."

The pro-competition strategy has assembled a catalog of failure in urban areas, a setting where the Managed Competition theory behind the Clinton plan is perhaps plausible. But in smaller cities and rural America, population is too sparse to support even the charade of competition. A town's only HMO or hospital cannot compete with itself. The minimum feasible size of a comprehensive HMO is 200,000 to 300,000 enrollees. Only 50% of the U.S. population lives in metropolitan areas able to support two or three HMOs, ie. with populations greater than 600,000. Yet even this population density does not guarantee real competition. Two or three HMOs that dominate a market will be tempted to collude in raising prices, enlarging the pie of health care dollars rather than fighting for the biggest piece. To quote J.K. Galbraith: "Oligopolies don't compete."

A Bureaucrat's Bonanza

According to the General Accounting Office, a Canadian-style, single-payer system would save enough on administrative overhead to cover all of the uninsured and eliminate all co-payments and deductibles. The single payer approach would sharply cut the $50 billion spent annually on insurance overhead by eliminating marketing costs, efforts at selective enrollment, stockholder's profits, executives' exorbitant salaries, and lobbying expenses. In contrast, Clinton's plan would *increase* administrative costs, since savings from the planned computerization and standardization of billing would be dwarfed by the added costs of private insurance and Health Alliance bureaucracies.

By 1995, Clinton plans to ship nearly $300 billion annually in new business to private insurers whose overhead averages 14%. Current Medicaid enrollees would be shifted out of a public program with overhead of only 4% (Canada's program runs for less than 1% overhead), increasing insurance overhead by $21.9 billion. In addition, at present private insurers take no overhead from the care received by the uninsured; at 14% overhead, private insurers would reap another $9.5 billion annually for administering the coverage for the newly insured. Hence, insurance overhead costs for these two groups would rise by $31.4 billion. Insurance overhead would likely rise even more steeply as states opt to fold Medicare (whose current overhead is 2%) into the Alliances, and as Clinton's proposed tax subsidies stimulate the purchase of private long term care insurance.

Moreover, Clinton's Managed Competition plan would add yet another layer of bureaucracy—the Health Alliances. Instead of buying coverage directly from an insurer/HMO, most businesses and individuals would pay into a Health Alliance, which would contract with insurers, which would contract with doctors and hospitals. The pattern familiar from each attempted reform of the health insurance system over the past quarter-century seems likely to recur. New bureaucrats will join rather than replace their predecessors.

The bureaucratic tasks assigned to the Health Alliances are daunting. They will administer the Rube

Goldberg system of premium caps; negotiate with and monitor health plans for quality of care, risk selection and financial abuses; set fees and capitation payments; collect premiums from millions of employers and hundreds of millions of individuals; and verify eligibility for premium subsidies available to the 45.6 million people whose incomes are at or below 150% of poverty. For each low income family they will obtain an income estimate to establish presumptive eligibility, and then at the end of the year examine tax and other records to retroactively adjust the subsidy. Moreover, the Health Alliances are charged with ranking the quality of plans, though first they'll have to figure out how to accurately measure quality using data provided mainly by the plans themselves.

Strikingly, the elaborate and probably unworkable budgeting scheme would cap only employers' and government's costs, not patients'. Only the faintest restrictions would limit spending for co-payments, deductibles, uncovered services and supplemental coverage. Predictably, these unrestricted costs would balloon as providers compensate for any income lost due to budgetary caps. The net effect: costs will shift but continue to grow.

Clinton's advisors argue that administrative costs would be cut by winnowing the insurance industry to a few mega-firms, mandating electronic billing, and consolidating small group and individual policies that have traditionally had high overhead costs. But big insurance firms' overhead is as high as small ones'. The larger insured-group size may indeed lower insurance company overhead but only because the Health Alliances would take over the task (and expense) of assembling the groups. Electronic billing saves little for insurers, who are already largely computerized, and only a pittance for hospitals and doctors. (Bush's HHS Secretary, Sullivan, claimed potential savings totaling only $8 billion over 5 years.)

Overall, Clinton's plan would add substantial administrative tasks to the current system, and strengthen the position of insurance companies by greatly increasing their revenues and their leverage over providers. Only wishful thinking can project that insurance firms will use their increased power to lower their rakeoff, contained in their overhead costs.

The single payer approach would save additional billions on hospitals' and physicians' billing—Managed Competition, virtually none. The Canadian system pays hospitals on a lump sum basis, like a fire department in the U.S., eliminating per-patient billing, and hence the need to attribute costs for each aspirin tablet to individual patients and insurers. As a result Canadian hospitals spend little on billing and internal cost tracking, and less than 10% of their total budgets on administration; U.S. hospitals spend 24.8%. Winnowing the number of insurers to a handful would save little on hospital billing, and nothing on internal cost tracking. Most savings come in the move from two insurers to one. For instance, Hawaii, with only two private insurers has the highest hospital administrative costs in the nation. Moreover, intensifying insurers' oversight of clinical practice, as promised by Managed Competition, would increase the bureaucratic burdens for most hospitals and doctors. The Mayo Clinic already employs 70 full time people just to talk on the phone with managed care utilization reviewers.

Because it bypasses administrative savings, health planning, and effective budgeting, Clinton's plan will not contain costs and hence cannot expand coverage.

Sham Choices

The president's claim that his proposed reform would broaden Americans' health care choices is deceptive. His plan would obliterate the non-HMO and small scale providers that patients prefer, leaving Americans to choose from a menu offering only corporate care served up by insurance giants.

Clinton hopes to control costs through the rapid expansion of large HMOs, supposedly competing. But contrary to his assurances that other health insurance options will remain available, small scale, non-HMO practices cannot possibly coexist with a dominant HMO sector. Big HMOs skimp on doctors, employing about 1 physician for every 800 enrollees, often meaning long waits for hurried consultations. In contrast, the U.S. physician to population ratio is 1:400. Hence, HMO expansion would absorb many patients but few physicians. The result: a glut of doctors (mostly specialists) in non-HMO practice serving a shrinking pool of patients. Initially, doctors might increase fees to meet their overhead and maintain their incomes, but increasing fees would accelerate the movement of patients into HMOs.

If half of Americans enrolled in HMOs with 1 doctor per 800 enrollees (and competitive pressures would drive HMOs to keep physician staffing to the minimum) each non-HMO physician would serve an average of only 267 patients, too few to cover even office overhead. At some point non-HMO practices would collapse. At the limit, if all Americans enrolled in HMOs, about 275,000 doctors, most of them specialists, would be stranded in a non-HMO sector devoid of patients. Competition for HMO jobs would be fierce; the disruption of care massive.

The president's spin doctors portray his proposal as assuring a pluralistic health care system; patients choosing the kind of care they want, and doctors free of micro management. But simple calculations belie this image. Instead, a few insurance giants would dictate care.

The rosy image of universal coverage by clones of today's best non-profit HMOs is hardly germane. Managed Competition cannot mean top quality consumer-responsive plans like Group Health Cooperative of Puget Sound (GHC), nor even Kaiser, for everyone. These HMOs may produce one-time savings, but they haven't slowed the rate of growth of health costs. Managed Competition means far more stringent limits on care, and attention focussed on the bottom line rather than the patient. Undistinguished doctors who prescribe low cost care will be HMO favorites; superb but less frugal clinicians, will be unemployable. One example: Massachusetts' BayState HMO, facing financial failure, suddenly fired hundreds of psychiatrists. Their patients were instructed to call the HMO's 800 number and describe their psychiatric difficulties; a new mental health provider would be assigned. This in an HMO serving middle class patients.

Medicaid patients and others relegated to the lowest tier of HMO care will surely fare much worse. As Medicaid proves, a comprehensive benefit package is scant guarantee of quality or even access. Even in the best HMOs, sick, low income patients do poorly, according to the Rand Experiment. Forcing patients to pay steeply to avoid the cheapest plan is Clinton's central cost control tenet. The undoubted result: a bottom tier for those formerly uninsured or on Medicaid; a small step up for many low income workers; and multiple ascending tiers above. Those unable to buy their way up will be relegated to long waits, hurried care, shoddy facilities, and clinical decisions driven by cost consciousness. Medicaid mills are the working model; promised quality monitoring a sham. Health care quality measurement is a nascent science, decades away from reliable rankings of excellence.

Soak the Poor, Spare the Rich

For low and middle-income Americans Clinton would add the injury of regressive financing to the insult of sham choice. Employer-paid premiums are effectively deducted from employees' wages. By mandating a fixed per-employee contribution, the president would assure that a millionaire CEO bears the same deduction for insurance as his $20,000 per year secretary. In contrast, with a 5% payroll tax the millionaire would forfeit $50,000 in income, his secretary $1,000. (Income tax funding would produce an even more progressive gradient.) Indeed, the employer mandate in Clinton's plan would likely increase the overall regressivity of health care funding. Many of the uninsured who now receive some free care (effectively a subsidy from the affluent) would see their wages fall to cover their employers' new health insurance costs. For the average uninsured family care would increase modestly but costs would jump sharply.

Moreover, the poor would face staggering out-of-pocket cost even for covered services, as much as 20% of total income. There would be no subsidies available to help with co-payments. Hence, even in the "low-cost plan" a child requiring weekly allergy shots could easily cost a family $750 annually. Add to this the employee's 20% share of the premium—while the employer's share is capped at between 3.5% and 7.9% of payroll, the employee's share is not—and total expenses for *covered services* could consume more than 25% of family income.

The regressive financing implicit in Clinton's mandated premiums (a tax on the working poor) and high out-of-pocket costs (a tax on the sick) would be instantly rejected if made explicit. He shies from "tax" funding not to avoid taxes, but to avoid fair taxes.

Regression to the Meanest

The president's plan has powerful appeal to big insurance firms, and to all whose inner voice whispers the same answer for every question: "the marketplace." In contrast, a single-payer system would evict the middle men and the profit motive from health care. For the average American, Clinton proposes worse care, less choice of provider, and higher costs. A single payer would mean better, more affordable care and unrestricted choice.

In Orwellian fashion the plan offers a "single payer option" that erects new obstacles to single payer reform, requiring even more federal government waivers than are currently needed and restricting employer-based funding. Clinton's promises of easily available waivers are unlikely to bind future Republican administrations.

The Clinton plan would install insurance giants as the feudal lords of medicine. Measured by cost containment and access the plan would fail, and fail quickly. But it would make the terrain for reform more arduous. Republicans would point to yet another failed liberal program based on government intervention; Democrats would retreat to defense of the plans' few progressive shards, a reprise of their 1980s performance defending Medicaid, the worst health program in the developed world.

More important, the shift to outright ownership of health care by big insurers would thwart reform. At present, money flows through insurers' coffers to pay for care, but they don't yet own the hospitals and laboratories, or employ the doctors and nurses. We could now construct a non-entrepreneurial, democratic health system largely by redirecting the money flows, causing little disruption (except in the insurance industry).

Once the Clinton plan is enacted, dislodging insurers will mean taking back the hospitals and practices they've bought with our mandated premiums and tax dollars. Reclaiming these resources for public service will be politically formidable, and expensive—we'll no doubt have to pay for them a second time. Moreover, the small scale care that most Americans prefer—the familiar receptionist answering the phone, the doctor able to schedule an extra long visit without checking with a manager—will be long gone, along with the vestiges of medicine as a calling, not just a job. Their resurrection will be more difficult than repurchasing the bricks and mortar.

The Art of the Impossible

Following habit, the media portrays a bipartite health policy choice—the Democrats or the Republicans—omitting the most popular option, "None of the Above." Needing the support of progressives in his party, Clinton borrows single payer images and rhetoric, though little else. His obfuscation threatens to blunt grass roots mobilization, and ultimately to tar us with his failure.

As expected, many Washington leaders from the single payer ranks have fallen in behind the president—Congresspeople, union officials, even Citizen Action and Consumer's Union. But few of their troops follow. For Washington politicos each issue is a prelude to the next. The key question: Have I squandered or increased my political capital, my chances to move on and up? This spring, the AFL's health policy director slid easily into leadership of the HMOs' trade association; Citizen Action's chief moved to a job selling the Clinton plan for the Democratic National Committee. Even the more altruistic insiders fear that marginalization in the Washington health care debate will foreclose influence on future important issues.

But to caregivers and our patients, health care is *the* issue. Twenty years from now, god willing, we'll still be practicing medicine. Our colleagues and patients will little note our political clout, but long remember whether we steered them wrong or told the truth.

Our tasks

- To explain where Clinton's plan really leads, expose his rhetoric, and reach out to our communities who can pull erstwhile Washington allies back to the single payer camp.

- To assure, should Clinton have his way, that most will know that his failure is not ours. The fragments of his plan likely to pass—some insurance reforms and regulation, group purchasing pools, privatization of Medicaid, and incentives towards HMOs—will end neither the crisis nor the debate. Acquiescing now in unhealthy compromise will assure that Clinton's plan, once failed will push debate still further to the right. Proclamation of our salutary approach, even as we criticize the Clinton plan, lays the groundwork for future progress.

- To keep before America an alternative vision of health care guided by cooperation and public service, not competition and private gain.

This is an appropriate time to take stock of our victories and plot future ones. By mouthing our rhetoric the president has given single payer activists sincere flattery, and evidence of immense influence in shaping debate. Ten years ago, even liberal wisdom labeled universal coverage an intemperate demand, and urged acceptance of an agenda aspiring to defend Medicaid for the poor. Had single payer activists acquiesced, we might today be debating tax credits with a Republican president. Washington does not lack for leaders in compromise, but wants for leaders in principle.

Details of the Clinton Plan

Under the proposal the federal government would define a standard benefit package. States would certify insurance plans (mainly HMOs) authorized to offer this coverage, and would establish a single "Health Alliance" in each region to contract with the plans on behalf of small employers, the self-employed and unemployed (including current Medicaid recipients). Large employers could self-insure, contract directly with certified plans for coverage, or elect to pay into the Health Alliances.

The proposed benefit package includes comprehensive acute care coverage except for mental health, and adult dental and eye care. It would cover little nursing home care, and limited home care. Rehabilitation service would only be covered if functional improvement was demonstrable after 60 days. HMOs would charge a $10 fee for outpatient visits, $25 for an emergency room visit, and $5 per prescription. Out-of-pocket costs for the covered services would be capped at $1,500 per individual and $3,000 per family. Psychotherapy and substance abuse visits would require a $25/visit copayment, and be limited to 30 visits per year. (There would be no limits, and lower copayments for brief visits to prescribe and monitor psychiatric medications.) Inpatient psychiatric and substance abuse care would be limited to 30 days per episode and 60 days per year.

Health Alliances would also offer fee-for-service coverage, though in many areas this option would probably disappear because few physicians could maintain practices independent of the HMOs. Patients electing a fee-for-service plan would pay out-of-pocket for the first $200/$400 (individual/family) of care, the first $250 of prescription drugs, and 20% of all subsequent bills. Out-of-pocket caps similar to those in the HMO option would apply. Psychotherapy visits would be subject to a 50% copayment, and mental health benefits would be limited as under the HMO plan. The Health Alliance would set all fees under the fee-for-service plan, and ban balance billing.

A third coverage option would offer benefits similar to the HMO coverage when a patient used the HMO's doctors and facilities. Out-of-plan services would be subject to the same fees, copayments and deductibles as under the fee-for-service plan.

Who Would Pay the Premiums?

Employers would be required to pay 80% of the average cost of coverage, either to a Health Alliance or (for large firms) directly to the insurer. This employer contribution would be capped at 7.9% of payroll, with lower caps for small and low-wage employers. Employers could pay for more generous coverage, but eventually this extra payment would be counted as taxable income for the employee. Most people who elected a more expensive plan would have to bear the full additional cost themselves. Conversely, those choosing cheaper than average plans would pay less than 20% of the premium.

Medicaid (which would be limited to AFDC and SSI recipients) would pay over most monies to the Health Alliances which would enroll recipients in low-cost private plans. Medicaid would continue to cover services that are included under the current Medicaid plans but excluded from the standard benefit package (eg. first dollar coverage of prescription drugs).

The self-employed and unemployed would buy coverage through their Health Alliance, with subsidies for those with incomes below 150% of the poverty line.

States could fold Medicare into the Health Alliance contracting system, or leave it as a separate program. Prescription drug coverage would be added to Medicare in 1996.

Regulating the Plans

Insurance plans accepting any new enrollees would have to take all comers during the yearly enrollment period, and pre-existing conditions would be covered. The Health Alliances would pay health plans more for older and sicker patients, and would attempt to prevent even indirect methods of risk selection (eg. selective marketing to the healthy, or locating facilities only in low-risk areas).

The Health Alliances would charge patients and employers a community rate, adjusted only for family size. That is, the Health Alliance would charge a 60-year-old diabetic and a health 20-year-old the same amount to enroll in HMO A, even though the Health Alliance would pay the HMO much more for the diabetic.

Insurers could offer supplemental policies to cover services not included in the standard package, as well as co-payments and deductibles, but coverage duplicating the standard package would be banned. The federal government would specify 2 standard medigap policies that the fee-for-service plans sold through the Alliances would have to offer to all members during the annual enrollment period.

The plan specifies a complex regulatory structure to assure that premiums for the standard benefit package are limited (premium caps and budget regulations would not apply to supplemental coverage, out-of-pocket costs, and uncovered services). Initially, a national board would calculate a maximum premium target for each Health Alliance, based on the number, age and health status of the individuals covered, and the current costs of care in the region. Each Health Alliance would negotiate premiums with each insurer, and estimate how many Alliance members will sign up with each plan. If the total expected premiums exceeded the Alliance's premium cap, the Alliance would calculate the actual premiums paid, which would serve as the basis for calculating future years' premium caps. In each subsequent year the Alliance's premium cap would increase by a limited inflation factor, and be adjusted for demographic changes and to decrease regional variation. In order to stay within the premium cap, Alliances could freeze enrollment in higher cost plans, decrease fees for health providers, or tax high cost plans. Large corporations who remain outside of the Health Alliances would be subject to similar regulation.

The Health Alliances are also responsible for monitoring the quality of care, disseminating information about the available plans, collecting premiums from employers and individuals, and administering the subsidies for low-income people. People could apply for subsidies during the enrollment period, or at other times if they had a change of circumstance (eg. job loss or divorce). They would submit an income estimate to the

Health Alliance, which would calculate a subsidy. At the end of the year, the Alliance would verify actual income from tax forms and other records, and retroactively adjust the subsidies.

Costs and Funding

The plan would be fully phased in during 1997. It envisions health care cost increases even greater than would occur without reform through 1997, but projects large savings in subsequent years as a result of enhanced competition among health plans, premium caps, cuts in Medicare and Medicaid, and positive economic repercussions from the reform.

Funding for the government's portion would come from several sources. A laundry list of Medicare changes are projected to cut spending by $124 billion between 1996 and 2000. Medicaid savings are expected to total $114 billion by 2000, in part from outright cuts, in part from the transfer of working Medicaid recipients into the employer mandate system. New taxes (mainly sin taxes) are slated to raise $105 billion. The plan projects that corporate and individual income tax receipts will increase by $51 billion as effective cost containment provisions leave more money in tax payers' pockets, increasing taxable incomes. Administrative savings are expected from electronic billing and the adoption of uniform claim forms and procedures.

Miscellany

The plan would provide incentives for primary care by phasing in a requirement that 50% of all residency training slots be allocated to family medicine, general internal medicine, and general pediatrics; and by tipping physicians' fee schedules in favor of primary care services. It would modestly expand the training of nurse practitioners and physician incentives. It includes incentives for rural practice and resource development, as well as targeted programs for underserved areas. Malpractice regulations would undergo modest reform.

Other provisions include: exclusion of undocumented immigrants from guaranteed coverage, though their employers would be required to pay the mandated premium. States could not regulate insurance premiums as they now often do, except through the Health Alliances' premium caps. Taxes levied by a Health Alliance on high cost plans in order to get under the premium cap would be returned to employers to defray their share of premiums, but not to individuals. Medical care for auto accidents and work related illnesses would be delivered through an individual's health plan, which would charge their auto or workmen's compensation insurer based on a fee schedule promulgated by the Alliance. Tax subsidies would be offered for private long-term care insurance policies.

Finally, in a single page the plan outlines an option for states to pursue a single payer system. However, states would be required to apply for several waivers from the federal government, and could not use revenues from employers to provide more comprehensive coverage than the federal benefit package. (It is not clear whether administrative savings could be used to improve benefits, or would have to be returned to employers.) Moreover, any employer-based funding would be locked into the highly regressive pattern of Clinton's managed competition plan.

Many Proposals—All Preserve Insurance and Managed Care Giants

MANAGED COMPETITION PROPOSALS

ENTHOVEN/JACKSON HOLE
(EMPLOYER MANDATE)

BUSH/CONSERVATIVE DEMOCRATS
(TAX INCENTIVES W/OUT MANDATE)

AMERICAN HOSPITAL ASSOCIATION
(HOSPITAL-BASED HMO's)

GARAMENDI/STARR
(TAX FINANCED)

CLINTON
(EMPLOYER MANDATE
+
PREMIUM CAPS)

Robert McNamara coined the term "Managed Competition" to describe his management style as president of Ford Motors, and later as Secretary of Defense during the Vietnam War. McNamara's Defense Department Deputy, Alain Enthoven, went on to a career as a Stanford Business School Professor and health economist. In the early 1980s Enthoven designed a plan to restructure health care, and in 1986 named it Managed Competition. Subsequently, he and former Nixon advisor Paul Ellwood convened in Jackson Hole a group of corporate leaders. With funding from big insurers, this Jackson Hole group fleshed out Enthoven's original concept, and laid the foundation for Clinton's proposal.

Enthoven would strengthen the role of insurance giants like Prudential and Aetna, who would own and operate the managed care networks that are the backbone of Managed Competition. Several variations on his scheme have been proposed. All would retain his emphasis on managed care, fostering the market dominance of large vertically integrated provider/insurer organizations similar to HMOs, and would establish health insurance purchasing agencies ("Health Alliances") to serve as middlemen for individuals and small businesses to purchase coverage and regulate insurers. Enthoven would require all employers to pay for 80% of the cheapest available HMO, and suggests lowering the minimum wage 8% to cushion the impact on employers. Clinton retained Enthoven 80% employer funding, omitted his minimum wage cut, and added a complex system of premiums caps and subsidies administered by the Health Alliances. The conservative Democrats' proposal would omit the employer mandate, and instead offer tax incentives to businesses and subsidies for the poor. Under liberal versions, such as those offered by California Insurance Commissioner John Garamendi, the Health Alliances would contract with private insurers for virtually all coverage, with most funding from payroll taxes.

Clinton Believes We Are
*Over*insured(!)

CLINTON'S PLAN
KEY FEATURES

- GOVERNMENT DEFINES STANDARD BENEFIT PACKAGE

- EMPLOYERS CONTRIBUTE FIXED AMOUNT, EMPLOYEES PAY FULL EXTRA COST OF BETTER PLANS

- "HEALTH ALLIANCES" SERVE AS MIDDLE-MEN BARGAINING WITH AND REGULATING INSURERS ON BEHALF OF SMALL FIRMS AND INDIVIDUALS, AND ADMINISTERING SUBSIDIES

- EXPAND COVERAGE THROUGH EMPLOYER MANDATE AND SUBSIDIES FOR PRIVATE COVERAGE

- REGULATION TO LIMIT PREMIUM INCREASES

Under Clinton's Plan the Federal Government would define a standard minimum benefit package. Large employers would contract for this coverage for their employees, and Health Alliances (HAs) would contract with private insurers on behalf of small employers, the self-employed and unemployed (including current Medicaid recipients, and, at the state's option, Medicare enrollees). Employers would pay 80% of the premium for a low cost plan (presumably a bare-bones HMO), with most individuals responsible for 20% of the low plans' premium, plus the full additional cost if they wanted better coverage, creating a steep financial penalty for choosing costlier alternatives.

The Health Alliances would use their market clout to drive down insurance prices, and would oversee the quality of care. They would enforce regulations attempting to prohibit risk selection, pre-existing condition exclusions, and other deleterious insurance company practices. They would also administer a complex system of premium caps designed to hold down costs if competition fails; collect premiums; and administer subsidies for low-income individuals and small business.

The Managed Competition theory behind Clinton's plan ascribes soaring costs to overinsurance. Americans, too insulated from the costs of care, are choosing to be profligate health care consumers. Hence they must be forced to be more cost conscious in purchasing insurance (by bearing the full extra costs of better coverage), and aided (through the HAs) in bargaining with insurers. The HAs would lean on the insurance companies/HMOs to lower premiums. They, in turn, would discipline doctors and hospitals by denying contracts to any who refused to comply with insurance company cost-cutting directives. Since a few managed care plans, giants like Aetna and Prudential, would enroll virtually all patients in a region, providers denied contracts would be forced out of business/practice, as would small insurers and HMOs. The belief in overinsurance remains unshaken by data showing that Americans pay the world's highest out-of-pocket costs, while receiving fewer doctor visits, hospital days, and even some types of transplants than do Canadians or people in several other nations with much lower health care costs.

Clinton's "Health Security" card is fitting symbol for an insurance company welfare scheme rhetorically disguised as health reform. Canadians' health cards entitle them to free care from any doctor and hospital they choose. Clinton's card would merely grant the right to buy restrictive partial coverage. Perhaps next he'll end hunger by distributing cards bestowing the right to buy food in a super market.

Perpetuating the Health Insurance Industry—and Crisis

CLINTON'S PLAN
A VISION OF THE FUTURE

- A FEW GIANT INSURERS/HMOs DOMINATE THE MARKET

- MOST PEOPLE FORCED INTO LOW COST PLANS

- DOCTORS EMPLOYED BY INSURERS/HMOs

- HOSPITALS CONTROLLED BY INSURERS/HMOs

- MULTI-TIERED CARE

- INCREASED BUREAUCRACY

- INEFFECTIVE COST CONTAINMENT

- REGRESSIVE FINANCING

Clinton's plan would push most Americans into restrictive managed care plans, owned by for-profit insurance companies. It would rob most patients of the right to choose, or change, their own doctor and hospital. Most doctors would become insurance company employees, some would probably be unemployed. Since only the wealthy could afford higher cost plans, Clinton's reform would assure a multi-tiered health care system, separate and unequal. In essence, his plan would perpetuate the private health insurance industry, the cause of the crisis, and complete the transformation of medicine from one-on-one doctor patient relationships to a medical system controlled by enormous corporate bureaucracies.

Moreover, there is no convincing evidence that Clinton's proposal could control health care costs since it relies heavily on a pro-competition, pro-managed care strategy that has failed in the past (see charts below). Administrative costs costs would actually rise under the president's plan. In addition, the President's plan would wipe out small insurers and fee-for-service practice, leaving a few giant plans and little competition. Already, 10 insurers control 70% of HMOs nationwide. Having muscled out competitors, the big insurers would enjoy a quasi-monopoly, foreclosing price competition. As Galbraith noted: "Oligopolies don't compete."

Clinton's financing proposal is extraordinarily regressive. It would force low and middle income Americans to pay dearly for their restrictive care. Employer-paid premiums are effectively deducted from employees' wages. Many would face staggering out-of-pocket costs even for covered services, as much as 20% of income. The regressive financing implicit in Clinton's mandated premiums (a tax on the working poor) and high out-of-pocket costs (a tax on the sick) would be rejected if made explicit. He shies from "tax" funding not to avoid taxes, but to avoid fair taxes.

Managed Care:
Part of the Problem,
Not the Solution

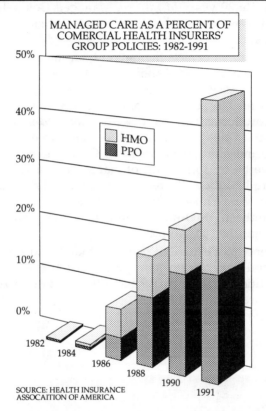

MANAGED CARE AS A PERCENT OF
COMERCIAL HEALTH INSURERS'
GROUP POLICIES: 1982-1991

HMO
PPO

SOURCE: HEALTH INSURANCE
ASSOCAITION OF AMERICA

Managed Competition has never worked anywhere. Its pro-managed care, pro-competition strategy represents merely an intensification of government and corporate policies that commenced with Richard Nixon's HMO act of 1973. Indeed, Paul Ellwood, convener of the Jackson Hole Group that is leading the charge to Managed Competition coined the term "HMO" in the early 70s, and personally sold Nixon on the concept as a counter to Ted Kennedy's single payer national health insurance proposal. Despite 20 years of failure, Managed Competition advocates see light at the tunnel's end, and suggest that we press on.

This graph depicts the rapid expansion of managed care in the past decade. About 40 million people are now enrolled in HMOs and more than half of all employees were covered by some form of managed care by 1993. Yet this growth has coincided with unprecedented cost increases. One-third of all Californians are enrolled in HMOs, and more than 80% of all California employees are covered by some form of managed care. Yet costs there are 19% above the national average and rising more rapidly. Massachusetts and Minnesota, the second and third highest HMO-penetration states, have similarly undistinguished cost records.

Hence past experience suggests that the expansion of managed care, a key component of the Managed Competition strategy, will have little affect on lowering health care costs.

HMOs
Haven't Contained Costs

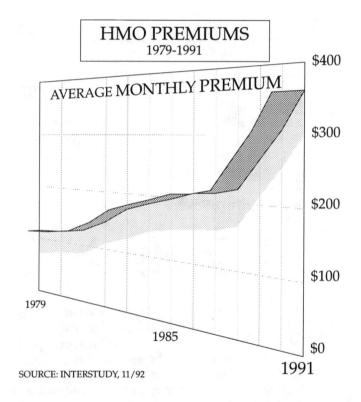

HMO PREMIUMS
1979-1991

AVERAGE MONTHLY PREMIUM

$400

$300

$200

$100

$0

1979

1985

1991

SOURCE: INTERSTUDY, 11/92

HMO premiums have more than tripled since 1979. There is little evidence to support the contention that expanding HMOs, a central feature of Managed Competition, will contain costs.

HMOs Offer No Clear Advantages in Rate of Premium Increase

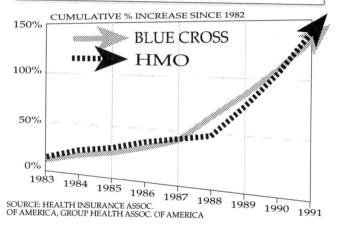

PREMIUM INCREASES SINCE 1982
BLUE CROSS vs. HMOs

CUMULATIVE % INCREASE SINCE 1982

BLUE CROSS
HMO

150%
100%
50%
0%

1983 1984 1985 1986 1987 1988 1989 1990 1991

SOURCE: HEALTH INSURANCE ASSOC.
OF AMERICA, GROUP HEALTH ASSOC. OF AMERICA

Nationwide, premiums for HMOs are rising at virtually the same rate as traditional Blue Cross and other indemnity insurers' premiums. Several recent reports have touted HMO cost savings because premium increases for 1992 were slightly lower than the increases for indemnity plans. Such short term trends should be interpreted cautiously. For instance, as this chart illustrates, between 1987 and 1988 HMOs' premium increases were much smaller than Blue Cross'. But in subsequent years HMO premiums increased more rapidly, canceling out the difference.

More HMOs Correlate
with *Greater* Cost Increases

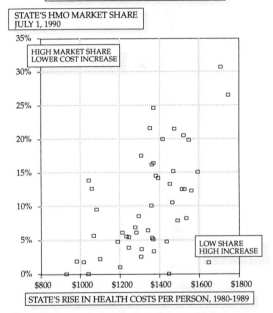

RISE IN HEALTH COSTS
COMPARED TO
HMO MARKET SHARE

STATE'S HMO MARKET SHARE
JULY 1, 1990

HIGH MARKET SHARE
LOWER COST INCREASE

LOW SHARE
HIGH INCREASE

STATE'S RISE IN HEALTH COSTS PER PERSON, 1980-1989

SOURCE: ACCESS & AFFORDABILITY MONITORING PROJECT,
BU SCHOOL OF PUBLIC HEALTH

This chart displays the relationship between the proportion of a state's residents enrolled in HMOs in 1990 and the state's increase in per capita health costs between 1980 and 1989. Each box represents a single state. Higher HMO market share correlated with greater cost increases, contradicting a central premise of Managed Competition theory—that pushing people into HMOs will control

217

costs.

While many HMOs offer lower premiums than competing indemnity insurers, this advantage is often due to risk selection (ie. enrolling healthier patients) and cost shifting onto other payers. In many cities, hospitals now give deeper discounts to HMOs than to Medicare, though HMO contracts forbid hospitals from disclosing their discounts, or complaining about them in public as they do about Medicare. Hospitals compensate for the discounts by raising rates for other patients.

HMOs Have Higher Insurance Overhead Costs

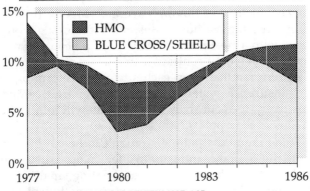

INSURANCE OVERHEAD, 1977-1986
BLUE CROSS/SHIELD VS. HMOs

- HMO
- BLUE CROSS/SHIELD

15%

10%

5%

0%

1977   1980   1983   1986

HEALTH CARE FINANCING REVIEW 1987; 6:35

According to the General Accounting Office, a Canadian-style, single payer system would save enough on administrative overhead to cover all of the uninsured and eliminate all co-payments and deductibles. The single payer approach would sharply cut the $50 billion spent annually on insurance overhead by eliminating marketing costs, efforts at selective enrollment, stockholder's profits, executives' exorbitant salaries, and lobbying expenses. In contrast, Managed Competition is likely to increase insurance overhead costs (as Enthoven forthrightly stated in the past). Current Medicaid enrollees would be shifted from a public program with overhead of 3.5%, to private insurance where overhead averages 14% (Canada's program runs for less than 1% overhead). All of the new coverage would be purchased from wasteful private insurers. As the graphs on this and the subsequent page show, administrative costs in managed care plans are no lower than in other forms of health insurance.

Moreover, Clinton's Managed Competition would add yet another layer of bureaucracy—the Health Alliances. Instead of buying coverage directly from an insurer/HMO, most businesses and individuals would contract with a Health Alliance, who would contract with insurers, who would contract with doctors and hospitals. The pattern familiar from each attempted reform of the health insurance system over the past quarter-century seems likely to recur. New bureaucrats will join rather than replace their predecessors.

Some argue that administration can be cut by winnowing the insurance industry to a few mega-firms, mandating electronic billing, and consolidating small group and individual policies that have traditionally had high overhead costs. But big insurance firms' overhead is as high as small ones'. The larger insured-group size may save insurance company overhead but only because the Health Alliances have taken over the task (and expense) of assembling the groups. Overall, Managed Competition would strengthen the position of insurance companies by greatly increasing their leverage over providers. Only wishful thinking can project that insurance firms will use their increased power to lower their rake-off, viz. overhead costs.

HMO Overhead Costs
Average 19%

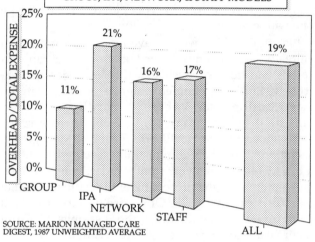

OVERHEAD COSTS OF HMOs–
A 1987 SURVEY
GROUP, IPA, NETWORK, & STAFF MODELS

OVERHEAD/TOTAL EXPENSE

GROUP 11%
IPA 21%
NETWORK 16%
STAFF 17%
ALL 19%

SOURCE: MARION MANAGED CARE
DIGEST, 1987 UNWEIGHTED AVERAGE

(CONTINUED FROM PREVIOUS PAGE)

The single payer approach would save additional billions on hospitals' and physicians' billing—Managed Competition, virtually none. The Canadian system pays hospitals on a lump sum basis, like a fire department in the U.S., eliminating per-patient billing, and hence the need to attribute costs for each aspirin tablet to individual patients and insurers. As a result, Canadian hospitals spend little on billing and internal cost tracking, and less than 10% of their total budgets on administration; U.S. hospitals spend more than 24%. Winnowing the number

221

of insurers to a handful, as promised under Managed Competition, would save little on hospital billing, and nothing on internal cost tracking. Most savings come in the move from two insurers to one. Moreover, intensifying insurers' oversight of clinical practice, as promised by Managed Competition, would increase the bureaucratic burdens for most hospitals and doctors. The Mayo Clinic already employs 70 full-time people just to talk on the phone with managed care utilization reviewers.

Electronic billing would save little for insurers, who are already largely computerized, and only a pittance for hospitals and doctors. Bush's Health & Human Services Secretary, Sullivan, claimed potential savings totaling only $8 billion over 5 years. According to *Modern Healthcare* magazine (May 17, 1993:39) "A new report commissioned by the Healthcare Financial Management Association . . . predicts administrative savings of $1.9 billion to $4.5 billion each year from standardizing and completely automating the processing of the estimate 1 billion claims filed each year . . . Of course, the industry will have to invest big money to get those savings, $767 million per year initially according to HCFA figures."

Because it bypasses administrative savings, Managed Competition can only expand access by increasing health spending. Actuaries for the Health Care Financing Administration have estimated that universal, comprehensive coverage under Managed Competition would increase health spending by at least $100 billion annually.

Overheads and Profits
Swallow 18% to 25% of Revenues

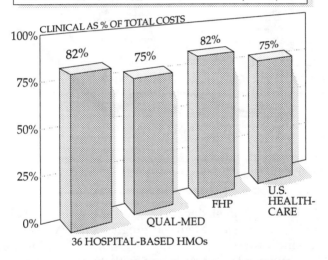

HMO MEDICAL COSTS
AS PERCENT OF TOTAL REVENUES, 1991/92

CLINICAL AS % OF TOTAL COSTS

100% —

82%   75%   82%   75%

75% —

50% —

25% —

0% —

36 HOSPITAL-BASED HMOs   QUAL-MED   FHP   U.S. HEALTH-CARE

SOURCE: MODERN HEALTHCARE 5/10/93 & HEALTH ECONOMICS 1993;2:13

This chart displays data on the proportion of HMOs' premiums devoted to clinical costs (i.e. costs other than overhead and profits) based on a survey of 36 hospital based HMOs, and the annual reports of three large for-profit HMOs. Overhead and profits consume between 18% and 25% of total HMO revenues, even higher than the 14% average for traditional insurance plans.

223

Federal Employees' Plan Is No Model for Containing Costs

FEDERAL EMPLOYEES HEALTH BENEFIT PLAN
VS.
OVERALL HEALTH COSTS

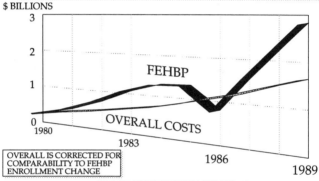

SOURCE: CONGRESSIONAL RES SVC, 1989-

Over the past decade a growing number of big employers and state Medicaid programs have engaged in the kind of hard bargaining envisioned for Managed Competition's Health Alliances, with no noticeable effect on health care costs. The Federal Employee Health Benefits Program (FEHBP), has been touted by the Heritage Foundation and others as a model for Managed Competition. Most enrollees have switched from fee-for-service to managed care plans. Yet, the FEHBP has averaged double digit rate increases since 1984; its costs rose faster in the 1980's than overall health care costs, according to data from a Congressional Research Service study.

Managed Competition:
Health Will Depend on Wealth

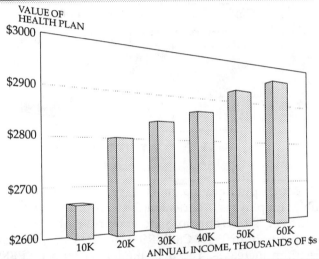

MULTITIERED CARE IN THE FEHBP:
INCOME AND HEALTH PLAN VALUE

SOURCE: CRS, MAY 24, 1989, 1988 FED EMPLOYEES HEALTH BENEFITS PROGRAM DATA.
DATA SHOWN FOR EMPLOYEES AGE 45-49, OTHER AGES SHOW THE SAME TREND

Because the FEHBP fixes the government's contribution and requires employees to bear the full extra cost of better plans, the predictable income gradient has emerged in coverage; higher income workers have better health plans. Managed Competition incorporates almost identical incentives, assuring rigidly class-stratified care.

California Public Employee Plan Isn't a Good Model

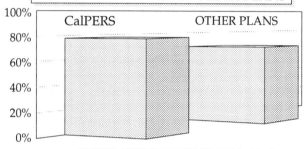

PREMIUM INCREASES, 1987-1991
CalPERS vs. OTHER CALIFORNIA PLANS

CalPERS   OTHER PLANS

100%
80%
60%
40%
20%
0%

SOURCE: SURVEY OF SEIU MEMBERS, 12/11/92

Much publicity has been given to the California Public Employees' Retirement System (CalPERS), Alain Enthoven's current favorite exemplar of Managed Competition. In 1993, CalPERS negotiated very modest premium increases. Yet, over the longer term CalPERS record is less encouraging; cost increases exceeded the national average for three of the last five years. As shown in this chart, members of the Service Employees International Union (SEIU) covered by CalPERS actually experienced larger health insurance cost increases than other SEIU members in California. Moreover, CalPERS' lower premium increases in the past two years may just mean that costs were shifted to employees via higher out-of-pocket costs, or to non-CalPERS insurance purchasers. Overall health care costs in California have been rising faster than the nationwide average.

HMOs
Don't Give Better Care

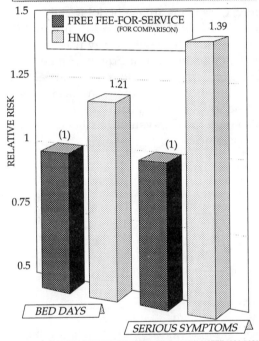

BED DAYS AND SERIOUS SYMPTOMS:
HMO CARE COMPARED TO FREE FEE-FOR-SERVICE

RELATIVE RISK

- FREE FEE-FOR-SERVICE (FOR COMPARISON)
- HMO

1.39

1.21

(1)

(1)

BED DAYS

SERIOUS SYMPTOMS

SOURCE: RAND HEALTH INSURANCE EXPERIMENT, LANCET 1986; i:1017

The effects of Managed Competition on the quality of care are uncertain. The Rand Health Insurance Experiment found that HMO patients suffered more serious symptoms and spent more days in bed than comparable patients randomized to fee-for-service care, without co-payments. This finding is particularly disturbing because the HMO studied, Group Health Cooperative of

Puget Sound, is widely considered among the nation's best.

The Rand study was carried out in the 1970s, but remains the only randomized trial of HMO vs. fee-for-service care. All of the more recent studies of quality of care in Managed Care plans are methodologically weak. There are virtually no data on outcomes under Managed Competition. The FDA would surely reject a pharmaceutical firm's application for approval of a new drug if it were presented with such poor and partial data. Yet, President Clinton would commit the health care of 250 million Americans to this untried approach. In contrast, Canada's single payer system has been proven by 25 years of experience.

Patients Prefer Small Doctors' Offices, But Clinton Proposes Massive HMOs

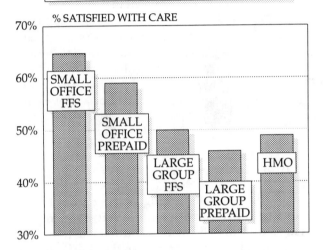

PATIENT SATISFACTION WITH CARE:
HMOs VS. DOCTOR'S OFFICES

% SATISFIED WITH CARE

SOURCE: JAMA 1993: 270:835.

A recent survey of over 17,000 people found that patients were more satisfied with their care in small offices than in large clinics or group practices, and rated care higher when their doctor was paid a fee-for-service rather than on a capitation or prepaid basis., as in HMOs. Ironically, these survey findings appeared just before President Clinton announced his plan, which would virtually wipe out the small-scale, non-HMO practic that most patients clearly prefer.

Managed Care Works Worst for Those Who Are Poor and Ill

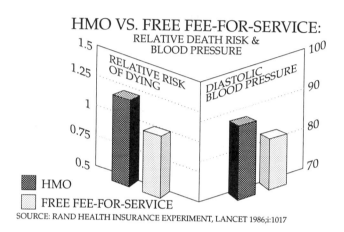

HMO VS. FREE FEE-FOR-SERVICE: RELATIVE DEATH RISK & BLOOD PRESSURE

RELATIVE RISK OF DYING

DIASTOLIC BLOOD PRESSURE

■ HMO
☐ FREE FEE-FOR-SERVICE

SOURCE: RAND HEALTH INSURANCE EXPERIMENT, LANCET 1986;i:1017

A particularly disturbing finding from the Rand Health Insurance Experiment is that poor, high risk patients fared poorly when randomized to an HMO. Diastolic blood pressure and overall risk of dying were both significantly higher in the HMO enrollees than in those receiving fee-for-service care with comprehensive coverage similar to Canada's. In contrast, wealthy patients appeared to do well in this excellent HMO (Group Health Cooperative of Puget Sound).

Unfortunately, poor patients are the ones most likely to be forced into managed care plans under Clinton's proposal, and plans are apt to be of far lower quality than Group Health Cooperative.

Most Americans Don't Live in an Area Dense Enough to Support Competition

Figure 1. Health Markets with Populations ≥360,000 in the United States.
Metropolitan areas (health markets) with populations ≥360,000 are shown in black.

Source: NEJM 1993; 328:148.

Where is Competition Feasible? In smaller cities and rural America, population is too sparse to support even a semblance of the competition fundamental to Managed Competition's cost control strategy. A town's only HMO or hospital cannot compete with itself. The minimum feasible size of a comprehensive HMO is about 400,000 enrollees. While it is unclear how many overlapping HMOs are needed to foster real competition, three competitors in the same area is probably a minimum. (More may be needed. J.K. Galbraith has noted that oligopolies don't compete. Three HMOs that dominate a region may tacitly collude to drive up prices, enlarging the pie of health care dollars rather than fighting for the biggest piece.) In order to support three comprehensive HMOs a market area's population must exceed 1.2 million. Yet only 42% of the U.S. population lives in metropolitan areas of this size. Twenty-six of the 50 states have no one market area with a population greater than 1.2 million.

Even assumptions much more sympathetic to Managed Competition suggest that this strategy is inapplicable in much of our nation. On the map shown on the previous page, market areas with populations greater than 360,000 are shaded black. For the 36% of Americans who live in the unshaded areas (including 9 entire states), competition among health care providers is inconceivable.

Managed Competition: Incentives to Avoid Treating the Sick

"Information technology...makes mass clinical audit possible, so that practice in whole populations can for the first time become routinely self-critical, and care can begin to merge with science. This requires that audit data be used only to discover the truth, not to reward or punish competing entrepreneurs whose incomes depend on the data they record. Without this guarantee, audit data will be as close to the truth as a tax return. "

~*Julian Tudor Hart*

SOURCE: HART JT. LANCET 1992; II:772

Managed Competition advocates argue that the Health Alliances' oversight will assure that managed care plans compete based on quality and efficiency. The quote reproduced above underlines the distortion that occurs when clinical records are used as the basis of financial reward or punishment.

Quality is rarely directly measured. More often, surrogate yardsticks are used that can be circumvented by clever or unscrupulous entrepreneurs. An old Soviet cartoon is apropos. The beaming workers at a nail factory are pictured with a plaque commending them for meeting their 1000 ton monthly quota, while next to them sits the single giant nail they made. Low surgical mortality can be achieved by superb technique, or by refusing to operate on sick patients.

Since 10% of the population consumes 72% of health care, the easiest way for insurers/HMOs to undercut their competitors' prices while producing "superior outcomes" is to quietly avoid enrolling sick people in the first place, and drive away the chronically ill by offering unsatisfactory care. Immense financial reward accrues to insurers that successfully avoid risk, assuring extraordinary efforts to circumvent regulatory bans on risk selection. Requirements for open enrollment are easily subverted. Place sign-up offices on upper floors of buildings with malfunctioning elevators. Refuse contracts to providers convenient to neighborhoods with high rates of HIV (an example of medical redlining). Structure salary scales to encourage a high turnover among physicians; the longer they're in practice, the more sick patients they accumulate. Assure the easy availability of services for the worried well, and inconvenience for those with expensive chronic illnesses. In Medicare's HMO Demonstration Project, regulatory oversight did not avert even flagrant abuses. Predictably, the Health Alliances' efforts to adjust the capitation fee for predictors of health risk will be no match for the creative and subtle means devised by unscrupulous insurers/HMOs to avoid the sick. In a competitive environment, insurers that lower their costs by effectively dodging health problems are sure to succeed, those that tackle them are likely to fail.

There is a dismal record of failure at even the narrow task of regulating insurers' financial dealings. Effective audits of the largely insurer-supplied regulatory data are rare. About half of all state insurance commissioners were previously employed by insurance firms, and half are employed by insurers after leaving office. Several big insurers (eg. Maxicare and W. Virginia Blue Cross) have collapsed under regulators' noses, leaving thousands of patients and providers high and dry. While New York's Empire Blue Cross teetered at the edge of bankruptcy it shipped millions to a computer novice board member for the development of a massive claims processing system; spent lavishly on office decor and helicopter rides; and, after gaining approval for a huge rate increase, voted executives retroactive pay raises. All this in a state better equipped than most to regulate insurers. The Health Alliances' tasks will be far broader and more difficult, and the pressures they face far greater.

Big Profits for Big Companies

HMOs:
THE INDUSTRIALIZATION OF CARE

"(HMOs) could stimulate a course of change in the health industry that would have some of the classical aspects of the industrial revolution - conversion to larger units of production, technological innovation, division of labor, substitution of capitol for labor, vigorous competition, and profitability as the mandatory condition of survival."

~Paul Ellwood

SOURCE: HEALTH MAINTENANCE STRATEGY. MED CARE 1971; 9:291.

This quotation is reproduced from Paul Ellwood's 1971 paper proposing the cultivation of managed care. Ellwood coined the term "HMO", and convinced Richard Nixon to adopt a pro-HMO strategy as a counter to the movement for national health insurance in the early 1970s. More recently Ellwood convened "The Jackson Hole Group" in his living room in Wyoming. This collection of insurance executives, corporate leaders and their policy advisors has played a key role in lobbying for Managed Competition.

Ellwood's words portray his vision of a health care system owned and operated by a few huge corporations competing for profits.

Forcing Doctors Out of Work

"(Managed Competition) will put a lot of specialists out of work.... For some, it will become virtually impossible to practice in certain communities because nobody will want to hire you..."

~*Paul Ellwood*

SOURCE: JAMA 1993; 269:1604

Managed Competition would use a stick rather than a carrot to address the surplus of specialists in the U.S. Canada has emphasized the training of primary care physicians and appropriate fee schedules to address this issue.

The Clinton Plan:
Free Choice of Doctor
Only for the Wealthy

"What about traditional fee-for-service individuals and single-specialty group practices? We doubt they would generally be compatible with economic efficiency.... Some would survive in private solo practice without health plan contracts, serving the well-to-do."

~Enthoven & Kronick

SOURCE: NEJM 1989; 320:94.

In this quotation, Managed Competition's architects make clear their vision of the future. Private practice would shrivel. Only a few of the wealthy would retain a free choice of physicians.

Managed Competition Could Cause a Massive Disruption of Care

MANAGED COMPETITION
AND THE CRASH OF
FEE-FOR-SERVICE PRACTICE

▶ THE U.S. HAS ~1 MD PER 400 POPULATION.

▶ HMOs EMPLOY ~1MD PER 800 ENROLLEES.

▶ IF 50% OF AMERICANS ENROLLED IN HMOs, 1MD PER 267 PATIENTS REMAIN IN THE FFS SECTOR. FFS PRACTICE WOULD NOT BE VIABLE.

▶ IF 100% OF AMERICANS ENROLLED IN HMOs, ~ *275,000 PHYSICIANS WOULD BE STRANDED* IN A FFS SECTOR DEVOID OF PATIENTS.

Managed Competition proponents portray their proposals as assuring a pluralistic health care system—patients choosing the kind of care they want, and doctors free of government coercion. But simple calculations belie this image.

Managed Competition would foster the rapid expansion of HMOs that employ mainly salaried physicians (eg., the Kaiser or Harvard Community (HCHP) health plans). But a dominant HMO sector cannot possibly coexist with a viable fee-for-service sector. Kaiser, HCHP, and similar HMOs employ about 1 physician for every 800 enrollees, and most of these physicians are primary care practitioners. In contrast, for the nation as a whole the physician to population ratio is 1:400, and most physicians are specialists. Hence, the HMO expansion envisioned under managed competition would absorb relatively few physicians, mostly primary care doctors. This would leave a glut of specialists in the fee-for-service sector serving a shrinking pool of patients. Initially, fees might be increased to maintain physicians' incomes, but increasing fees would accelerate the movement of patients into HMOs.

If half of Americans enrolled in HMOs that maintained staffing patterns similar to Kaiser's, each remaining fee-for-service physician would serve an average of only 267 patients, too few to maintain a viable practice. At some point the fee-for-service sector would completely collapse, leaving tens of thousands of doctors who had not secured salaried positions in HMOs scrambling. At the limit, if 100% of patients were enrolled in Kaiser-like HMOs, about 275,000 doctors, most of them specialists, would be stranded in a fee-for-service sector devoid of patients. Competition for HMO jobs would be fierce. The disruption of care massive.

Doctors Outside HMOs Would be Forced to Charge Huge Fees

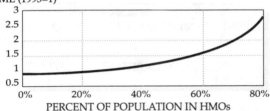

FEE-FOR-SERVICE COSTS MUST RISE
TO MAINTAIN MD's INCOMES
AS HMO ENROLLMENT GAINS

FEE INCREASE NEEDED TO MAINTAIN CONSTANT MD INCOME (1993=1)

PERCENT OF POPULATION IN HMOs

This graph illustrates an implication of the increasing glut of physicians in the fee-for-service sector as HMO enrollment increases under Managed Competition. The number of fee-for-service patients per physician would fall because expanding HMOs would absorb many patients but only a few physicians. Hence, in order to maintain constant incomes for the many physicians left in fee-for-service practice, the total physician fees per patient would have to grow to astronomical levels.

For example, Princeton Health economist Uwe Reinhardt has calculated (Health Economics 1993; 2:7-14) that if 50% of Americans enrolled in Kaiser-like HMOs, physician costs for the 50% remaining in the fee-for-service sector would have to total $3,000 per family in order to maintain current physician income levels. By contrast, current average per-family spending for physicians' fees totals about $1,600.

Managed Competition:
A Grimm Fairytale

CLINTON'S PLAN
CAN IT WORK?

- LIMITS PATIENTS' FREEDOM TO CHOOSE THEIR DOCTOR

- HMOs/MANAGED CARE HAS NOT SLOWED COST GROWTH

- INCREASES BUREAUCRACY

- NO COMPETITION IN SMALL CITIES AND RURAL AREAS

- COMPLEX REGULATION OPENS LOOPHOLES FOR INSURERS

- CREATES NON-COMPETITIVE OLIGOPOLIES WITH PROFIT INCENTIVES TO LOWER QUALITY

Clinton's plan would sacrifice many patients' rights to choose their doctor, forcing them to pay dearly for any plan better than a stripped down HMO. It would ensconce a highly bureaucratic health care system, rigidly stratified by income. Its theoretical precepts are irrelevant to rural America and to small cities; half of our nation. Moreover, there is little evidence that this strategy would control costs.

The President's rosy image of universal coverage under clones of today's best HMOs is hardly germane. His plan cannot mean top quality plans for all, or even most. Good HMOs may produce modest one-time savings, but haven't slowed cost growth. The Clinton plan dictates harsher limits implemented through profit-driven insurers. Undistinguished doctors who prescribe low cost care will be HMO favorites; superb but less frugal clinicians, unemployable. Massachusetts' BayState HMO offers a glimpse of the Clintonian future. Responding to competitive pressures, this middle class HMO suddenly fired hundreds of psychiatrists. Their patients were to call an 800 number, describe their problems, and be assigned a new therapist. Low income patients stuck in bottom tier HMOs will fare worse. Financial barriers are Clinton's cure for the overinsurance and excessive choice that his theory blames for medical inflation. Those unable to buy their way up will be relegated to long waits, hurried care, shoddy facilities, and clinical decisions driven by cost consciousness.

A Canadian-style single payer system would save $100 billion annually on administrative overhead. Clinton's plan would increase administrative costs. In 1997 it would pump an additional $300 billion through private insurers (current overhead 14%). He would privatize Medicaid (current overhead 4%) and, in some states, Medicare (current overhead 2%). In addition, insurers would administer coverage for the newly insured, whose care now costs $34 billion (current overhead 0%). Overall, insurance overhead would rise by about $30 billion, dwarfing savings from computerization and standardized billing forms. (Bush's HHS Secretary estimated these savings at $8 billion over 5 years when he proposed this approach). Moreover, Clinton would add a new layer of bureaucracy - the Health Alliances - with daunting tasks: administer the Rube Goldberg system of premium caps; monitor health plans for quality, risk selection and financial abuses; set fees and premiums; collect funds from millions of employers and hundreds of millions of individuals; and means-test the 45.6 million low income people and millions of businesses eligible for subsidies. For each subsidized family, the Alliances would obtain an income estimate to establish presumptive eligibility, and at the end of the year examine tax and other records to retroactively adjust the subsidy.

Managed Competition:
Prudential's Choice

> "
> FOR (PRUDENTIAL) THE
> BEST-CASE SCENARIO FOR REFORM
> - PREFERABLE EVEN TO THE
> STATUS QUO - WOULD BE
> ENACTMENT OF A MANAGED
> COMPETITION PROPOSAL. "
>
> -BILL LINK
>   EXECUTIVE V.P.
>   PRUDENTIAL

SOURCE: PRUDENTIAL INSURANCE COMPANY NEWSLETTER, 1993

Managed Competition has powerful appeal to big insurance firms, and to all whose inner voice whispers the same answer for every question: "the marketplace." But no poll or survey shows a trace of grass roots support. Bill Clinton's pollster, Celinda Lake, summarized her focus groups' views of Managed Competition: "laughable." The powerful coalition advocating Managed Competition hopes to broker a deal: protect insurers and the most powerful providers, and shift costs from big business to small business and workers.

Managed Competition theory was honed by the Jackson Hole Group, a circle of insurance executives, business leaders, and conservative academics financed by hundreds of thousands of dollars of insurance company grants.

More recently, Aetna, Prudential, Cigna, Met Life and Traveler's have formed a new "Coalition for Managed Competition" to lobby for this reform strategy. These "Big 5" insurers, along with Blue Cross, stand to profit most under Managed Competition. Their financial clout will give them leverage to cut special deals with hospitals and doctors, wipe out competitors by undercutting their prices and absorbing temporary losses, and expand their market share.

"Are there several doctors in the house, so we can have a little managed competition?"

A *New Yorker* Critique

We cannot improve on the *New Yorker's* prose: "The pile of evidence that a single-payer system, in which the government serves as the insurance company—the Canadian system—works better than any other is by now so high that it is almost embarrassing . . . As the *Times* noted recently, 95% of Canadians report having received within 24 hours all the care they needed, and public support for the program remains at about 90%. Nor is this a case where you sacrifice efficiency for social welfare. (Even in *Barron's*, Wall Street's trade paper, it has been conceded blandly this week that Canadian health care costs are lower because a single-payer system is always more efficiently administered.) This is a case where you can have more, better, and cheaper, all at once.

"The political reason [why we won't get a Canadian-style system] is obvious. The people who would benefit from a Canadian-style system, which is to say just about everybody, don't have concentrated political power. Those who would lose, which is to say the insurance companies, are unapologetically prepared to do whatever it takes to make sure that health insurance will remain their monopoly. They'll spend hundreds of millions of dollars of their clients' money on ad campaigns (that is, scare stories with slogans) and political contributions.

"What we seem likely to get from the Clinton task force is some version of "managed competition", a pseudo-market system, which will probably institutionalize the insurance companies as the feudal lords of American medicine. Patients will be organized into big groups, in which they will most likely (in the case of the poor, quite certainly) have much less choice than they would have under a Canadian-style system. No one seriously expects that, given the quasi-monopoly that each organization will enjoy, there will be any serious price competition. When the Big Three ran the auto industry, they controlled prices very effectively, and no one imagines that compact health-care plans from Japan will ever penetrate (or even be allowed to enter) this market."

SYLVIA

by Nicole Hollander

Now that it's summer, Love Cop is busier than ever keeping incompatible couples apart.

Remember... Lust makes you stupid.

© 1993 BY NICOLE HOLLANDER

When I look into your eyes, I forget how nuts you are on the benefits of the Cana-dian-style single-payer health system over managed competition.

"Managed Competition"... featuring mandatory enrollment in super HMO's—your doctor and hospital chosen for you—an untried theory be-loved by insurance companies and heart-less bureaucrats... and yet you're so darn cute.

Please step away from each other now or I'll be forced to hurt you for your own good.

Nicole Hollander

Part X
A Force for Change:
Public Opinion
on Health Care Reform

The health insurance industry asserts that an NHP couldn't work in the U.S. because "Americans are much less tolerant of governmental control"than Canadians. Turning to facts, the overwhelming majority of Americans favor a Canadian-style plan. Conversely, most Canadians prefer their system to the current U.S. system; less than 5% would switch if given the choice. Many people think that doctors oppose a national health care program, but most American doctors favor such reform, and would even agree to a 10% pay cut to reduce the bureaucratic hassles they currently face. Even most health care economists favor the Canadian system.

Americans not only favor such a plan, but are strongly in favor of paying for it with taxes that would replace the current high-premium, inefficient system.

POTENTIAL SUPPORTERS

- The Uninsured (all would be covered)
- The Elderly & Middle Class (ends underinsurance)
- Medicaid Recipients (assures one class care)
- Big Business (contains costs)
- Physicians (helps patients, curtails bureaucracy)
- Union Workers (no bargaining for health benefits)

OPPONENTS

- Insurance Companies (lose business)
- Many Providers (fear change)
- Some Small Businesses (forced to pay a share)

The potential support for a national health program is broad because it would improve the coverage for virtually all Americans. The uninsured would be covered. Seniors and middle-class Americans who currently have policies requiring significant co-payments and deductibles, and which usually exclude key services such as nursing homes and prescription drugs, would gain comprehensive coverage. Medicaid recipients would see the end of their second-class status. Businesses would gain through the effective cost containment under a national health program. Physicians would suffer far less bureaucratic interference in the doctor/patient relationship, and would be relieved of enormous paperwork burdens. For unions, a national health program would remove a contentious, often unwinnable issue from collective bargaining. Eighty-nine percent of recent strikes have included health benefits as a primary issue.

Opposition to a national health program comes from a narrow but powerful group. The insurance companies would lose enormous revenues, and are spending vast sums to lobby aganinst a national health program. Some providers, particularly for-profit hospitals and physicians in the highest paid specialties, fear loss of income. And some small businesses oppose national health insurance because they would be forced to pay a share of health costs (currently about half of them offer no health benefits).

Insurance Industry Dominates the Boston Skyline

This picture illustrates the power of opponents of a National Health Program. It shows the two tallest buildings in Boston, the John Hancock Tower and the Prudential Center. At present, private insurers collect about $300 billion each year in health insurance premiums. The insurance industry would have little place in an efficiently run National Health Program. Indeed, much of the funding needed to expand care for the uninsured and underinsured would come from eliminating wasteful insurance paperwork. The president of the Health Insurance Association of America, Carl Schramm, told a Consumer Reports reporter that the fight against national health insurance is "a life and death struggle" for the insurance industry. The insurance industry has funded many "studies" attacking a national health program, as well as a multi-million dollar lobbying and publicity effort.

Most Americans Prefer the Canadian NHP

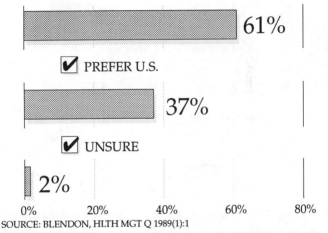

WOULD AMERICANS PREFER
THE CANADIAN NHP?

HARRIS POLL

(check one)

✔ PREFER CANADA

61%

✔ PREFER U.S.

37%

✔ UNSURE

2%

| 0% | 20% | 40% | 60% | 80% |

SOURCE: BLENDON, HLTH MGT Q 1989(1):1

"In the Canadian system of national health insurance, the government pays most of the cost of health care for everyone out of taxes, and the government sets all fees charged by doctors and hospitals. Under the Canadian system, people can choose their own doctors and hospitals. On the balance, would you prefer the Canadian system or the one we have here [in the U.S.]?" Sixty-one percent replied that they would prefer the Canadian system, 37% prefer the U.S. system, and 2% were unsure.

Fewer than 5% of Canadians want the U.S. System

WOULD CANADIANS PREFER
THE U.S. SYSTEM?

HARRIS POLL

(check one)

☑ PREFER U.S.

3%

☑ PREFER CANADA

95%

☑ UNSURE

2%

0% 10% 20% 30% 40% 50% 60% 70% 80% 90% 100%
SOURCE: BLENDON, HLTH MGT Q 1989(1):1

"In the U.S. system, the government pays most of the cost of health care for the elderly, the poor and disabled. Most others either have health insurance paid by their employers or have to buy it from an insurance company. Some have no insurance. Under the U.S. system people can choose their own doctors and hospitals. On balancc, would you prefer the U.S. system or the one we have here [in Canada]?" Three percent said yes. Two percent were unsure, and 95% said no. A Canadian colleague pointed out that this 3% figure is approximately equal to the illiteracy rate in Canada.

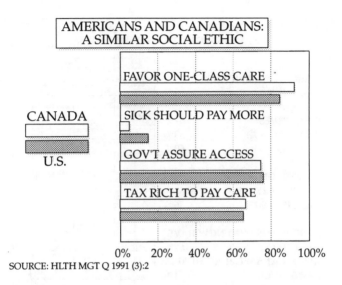

Contrary to Insurance Industry Claims about "Cultural Differences," Americans' Views Are Similar to Canadians'

AMERICANS AND CANADIANS:
A SIMILAR SOCIAL ETHIC

FAVOR ONE-CLASS CARE

CANADA

SICK SHOULD PAY MORE

U.S.

GOV'T ASSURE ACCESS

TAX RICH TO PAY CARE

0%   20%   40%   60%   80%   100%

SOURCE: HLTH MGT Q 1991 (3):2

The Harris polling organization surveyed Canadians and Americans about their attitudes towards health care. They expected to find substantial differences between the two nations that would account for the differences in the health care systems. To their surprise, more than 80% of the people in both countries favor one-class care, more than 75% believe that government should assure access to care, and about 66% advocate taxing the rich to pay for care. Fewer than 1 in 5 believe that the sick should pay more for care. The pollsters concluded that Americans and Canadians have very similar views of what a health care system should be, but that America's political leadership has not reflected the wishes of the American people.

U.S. Support for Canadian System Cuts Across Economic and Ethnic Lines

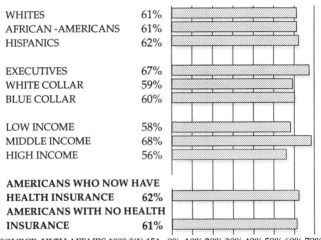

HOW MANY PREFER A CANADIAN-STYLE SYSTEM?
BY DEMOGRAPHIC GROUP, U.S., 1988

WHITES	61%
AFRICAN -AMERICANS	61%
HISPANICS	62%
EXECUTIVES	67%
WHITE COLLAR	59%
BLUE COLLAR	60%
LOW INCOME	58%
MIDDLE INCOME	68%
HIGH INCOME	56%
AMERICANS WHO NOW HAVE HEALTH INSURANCE	**62%**
AMERICANS WITH NO HEALTH INSURANCE	**61%**

SOURCE: HLTH AFFAIRS 1989;8(1):154   0% 10% 20% 30% 40% 50% 60% 70%

Support for a Canadian-style NHP is widespread. Majorities of virtually every demographic group support an NHP, in contrast to the more narrow support enjoyed by employer mandate programs. Under an NHP, most Americans' health coverage would improve because co-payments and deductibles would be eliminated and long-term care would be covered. Under employer mandate proposals the uninsured might gain coverage, but policies for most Americans would not be improved. As a result, virtually identical proportions of those with coverage and those currently uninsured support an NHP.

The Public Is Willing to Pay Taxes for Better Long-Term Care

PUBLIC OPINION ON LONG TERM CARE.

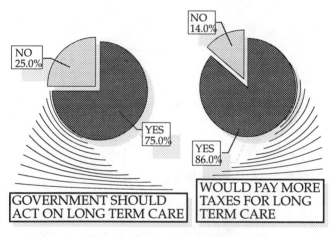

NO 25.0%

YES 75.0%

NO 14.0%

YES 86.0%

GOVERNMENT SHOULD ACT ON LONG TERM CARE

WOULD PAY MORE TAXES FOR LONG TERM CARE

SOURCE: R.L. ASSOC. 1987 AND L. HARRIS ASSOC. 1988

Public opinion strongly supports public financing of long-term care (LTC). Eighty-seven percent of Americans consider the absence of LTC financing a crisis; a majority prefer public over private funding. Federal administration is favored over private insurance programs by a 3 to 2 margin, and two-thirds believe that private insurance companies would undermine quality of care because of their emphasis on profits. 86% of Americans support government action for a universal long-term care program that would finance care for all income groups, and 75% would agree to increase taxes to fund it.

Dissatisfaction Is Rising

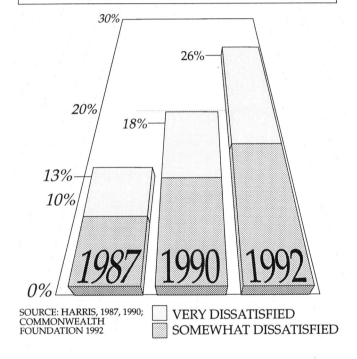

THE PERCENTAGE OF AMERICANS DISSATISFIED
WITH THEIR CARE HAS DOUBLED IN 5 YEARS

SOURCE: HARRIS, 1987, 1990;
COMMONWEALTH
FOUNDATION 1992

VERY DISSATISFIED
SOMEWHAT DISSATISFIED

According to polling data, the proportion of Americans who are somewhat dissatisfied or very dissatisfied with their medical care has doubled since 1987.

Americans Want Change

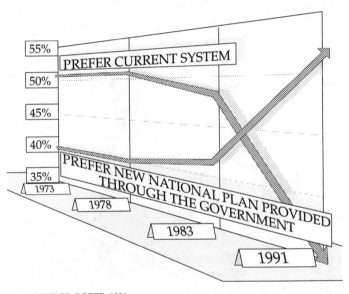

MANDATE FOR RADICAL CHANGE
IN HEALTH CARE, 1973-1990

55%

PREFER CURRENT SYSTEM

50%

45%

40%

35%

1973

PREFER NEW NATIONAL PLAN PROVIDED THROUGH THE GOVERNMENT

1978

1983

1991

SOURCE: ROPER, 1991

There has been a dramatic drop in the proportion of Americans who prefer the current system, and a substantial increase in those favoring a government funded national health insurance. This data is derived from repeated surveys by the Roper polling organization.

Higher Out-Of-Pocket Expenses Rejected as a Means to Control Costs

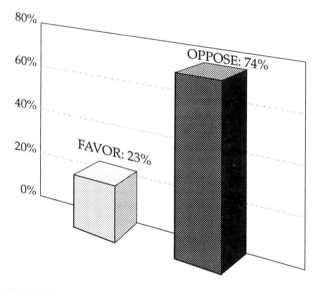

DO AMERICANS FAVOR HIGHER CO-PAYMENTS AND DEDUCTIBLES TO CONTROL COSTS?

OPPOSE: 74%

FAVOR: 23%

SOURCE: HEALTH AFAIRS, 1989;8(1):114

An overwhelming majority reject cost control strategies based on increasing patients' out-of-pocket costs. While many policy-makers think that Americans are "overinsured," and claim that co-payments and deductibles will solve the problem, the public thinks co-payments and deductibles are the problem.

Nearly 3/4 of Americans Want National Health Insurance

- **72%** Favor National Health Insurance

- **90%** of Blacks, 69% of Whites

- **79%** of Low Income, 66% of High Income

- **77%** of Democrats, 61% of Republicans

- **56%** Would prohibit paying extra for Better Care

- **84%** Would prohibit paying extra to avoid waiting in the doctor's office

- **30%** Favor expanding Medicaid for the poor

- **18%** favor expanding medicaid for the unemployed

A survey by the Arthur D. Little Corporation demonstrated that 72% of Americans favored national health insurance, including a majority of both Democrats and Republicans. It also found a remarkably egalitarian view of health care: 84% of Americans would prohibit paying extra to avoid waiting in a doctor's office, and 56% would prohibit paying extra for better care.

It is notable that less than one-third of Americans favored expanding Medicaid to cover the poor, and only 18% favored expanding Medicaid for the unemployed. These patchwork measures would benefit the uninsured, but would fail to address the problems faced by insured Americans. In contrast, a national health program would offer a solution for the insured as well as for the uninsured.

Most Doctors Side with the Public

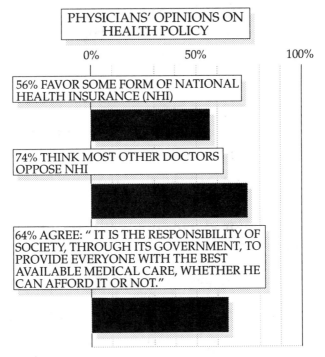

PHYSICIANS' OPINIONS ON
HEALTH POLICY

0%   50%   100%

56% FAVOR SOME FORM OF NATIONAL
HEALTH INSURANCE (NHI)

74% THINK MOST OTHER DOCTORS
OPPOSE NHI

64% AGREE: " IT IS THE RESPONSIBILITY OF
SOCIETY, THROUGH ITS GOVERNMENT, TO
PROVIDE EVERYONE WITH THE BEST
AVAILABLE MEDICAL CARE, WHETHER HE
CAN AFFORD IT OR NOT."

SOURCE: COLOMBOTAS & KIRCHNER -
PHYSICIANS AND SOCIAL CHANGE, 1986

A survey of physicians published in 1986 found that 56% favor some form of national health insurance, though about 74% of doctors think that most of their colleagues oppose such reform.

264

Canadian Physicians Wouldn't Want the U.S. System

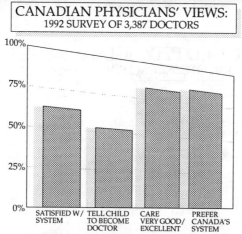

CANADIAN PHYSICIANS' VIEWS:
1992 SURVEY OF 3,387 DOCTORS

100%
75%
50%
25%
0%

SATISFIED W/ SYSTEM | TELL CHILD TO BECOME DOCTOR | CARE VERY GOOD/ EXCELLENT | PREFER CANADA'S SYSTEM

According to the *Toronto Globe and Mail*: "The most extensive survey of Canadian physicians ever conducted shows that the country's doctors are cheering up in the practice of medicine despite alot of bellyaching and predictions of dark days ahead.

"The Angus Reid survey, which recorded the views of 3,387 physicians for the weekly *Medical Post*, found that 63% were satisfied with their provincial medical plans, compared with a satisfaction level of 47% in a similar survey in 1979. . . . A majority, 52%, now say they would steer their children into medicine, compared with 44% in 1979.

"One percent of the doctors described Canada's system of health care as poor, while 83% perceived it as very good or excellent. . . . 71% of doctors reported that they were fairly or very satisfied with their incomes. The average net income of the respondents was $127,000 a year.

"About 85% agreed with the statement that the Canadian system is preferable to U.S. health care."

Most U.S. Doctors Would Accept a 10% Cut in Pay for Less Hassle

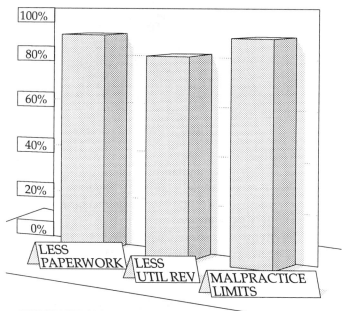

WOULD PHYSICIANS ACCEPT
10% LESS INCOME FOR LESS HASSLE?

SOURCE: METROPOLITAN LIFE SURVEY, 1991

The overwhelming majority of physicians would be prepared to trade 10% of their income for substantial decreases in paperwork and utilization review and for tort reform (malpractice limits).

Even Health Economists Favor Canada's System

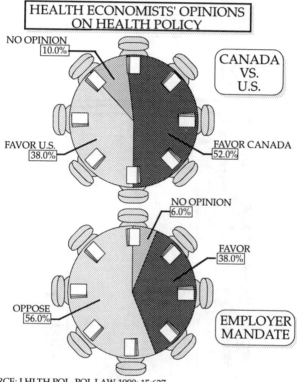

HEALTH ECONOMISTS' OPINIONS ON HEALTH POLICY

CANADA VS. U.S.

NO OPINION
10.0%

FAVOR U.S.
38.0%

FAVOR CANADA
52.0%

NO OPINION
6.0%

FAVOR
38.0%

OPPOSE
56.0%

EMPLOYER MANDATE

SOURCE: J HLTH POL, POL LAW 1990; 15:627

More than half of all health economists surveyed favor a Canadian-style NHP, whereas only 38% support an employer mandate approach similar to Clinton's plan.

267

SYLVIA

by Nicole Hollander

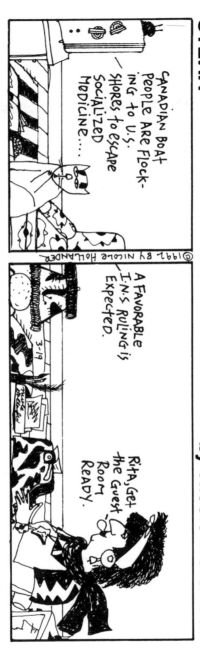

CANADIAN BOAT PEOPLE ARE FLOCK-ING TO U.S. SHORES TO ESCAPE SOCIALIZED MEDICINE....

A FAVORABLE I.N.S RULING IS EXPECTED.

RITA, GET THE GUEST ROOM READY.

Part XI

A National Health Program for the United States

A Physicians' Proposal

David U. Himmelstein, M.D.,
Steffie Woolhandler, M.D., M.P.H.,
and the Writing Committee
of the Working Group on Program Design*

Our health care system is failing. It denies access to many in need and is expensive, inefficient, and increasingly bureaucratic. The pressures of cost control, competition, and profit threaten the traditional tenets of medical practice. For patients, the misfortune of illness is often amplified by the fear of financial ruin. For physicians, the gratifications of healing often give way to anger and alienation. Patchwork reforms succeed only in exchanging old problems for new ones. It is time to change fundamentally the trajectory of American medicine—to develop a comprehensive national health program for the United States.

We are physicians active in the full range of medical endeavors. We are primary care doctors and surgeons,

*This proposal was drafted by a 30 member Writing Committee, then reviewed and endorsed by 412 other physicians representing virtually every state and medical specialty. A full list of endorsers is available on request.

psychiatrists and public health specialists, pathologists and administrators. We work in hospitals, clinics, private practices, health maintenance organizations (HMOs), universities, corporations, and public agencies. Some of us are young, still in training; others are greatly experienced, and some have held senior positions in American medicine.

As physicians, we constantly confront the irrationality of the present health care system. In private practice, we waste countless hours on billing and bureaucracy. For uninsured patients, we avoid procedures, consultations, and costly medications. Diagnosis-related groups (DRGs) have placed us between administrators demanding early discharge and elderly patients with no one to help at home—all the while glancing over our shoulders at the peer-review organization. In HMOs we walk a tightrope between thrift and penuriousness, too often under the pressure of surveillance by bureaucrats more concerned with the bottom line than with other measures of achievement. In public health work we are frustrated in the face of plenty; the world's richest health care system is unable to insure such basic services as prenatal care and immunizations.

Despite our disparate perspectives, we are united by dismay at the current state of medicine and by the conviction that an alternative must be developed. We hope to spark debate, to transform disaffection with what exists into a vision of what might be. To this end, we submit for public review, comment, and revision a working plan for a rational and humane health care system—a national health program.

We envisage a program that would be federally mandated and ultimately funded by the federal government but administered largely at the state and local level.

The proposed system would eliminate financial barriers to care, minimize economic incentives for both excessive and insufficient care, discourage administrative interference and expense, improve the distribution of health facilities, and control costs by curtailing bureaucracy and fostering health planning. Our plan borrows many features from the Canadian national health program and adapts them to the unique circumstances of the United States. We suggest that, as in Canada's provinces, the national health program be tested initially in statewide demonstration projects. Thus, our proposal addresses both the structure of the national health program and the transition process necessary to implement the program in a single state. In each section below, we present a key feature of the proposal, followed by the rationale for our approach. Areas such as long-term care; public, occupational, environmental, and mental health; and medical education need much more development and will be addressed in detail in future proposals.

Coverage

Everyone would be included in a single public plan covering all medically necessary services, including acute, rehabilitative, long-term, and home care; mental health services; dental services; occupational health care; prescription drugs and medical supplies; and preventive and public health measures. Boards of experts and community representatives would determine which services were unnecessary or ineffective, and these would be excluded from coverage. As in Canada, alternative insurance coverage for services covered under the national health program would be eliminated, as would patient co-payments and deductibles.

Universal coverage would solve the gravest problem

in health care by eliminating financial barriers to care. A single comprehensive program is necessary both to ensure equal access to care and to minimize the complexity and expense of billing and administration. The public administration of insurance funds would save tens of billions of dollars each year. The more than 1500 private insurers in the United States now consume about 8 percent of revenues for overhead, whereas both the Medicare program and the Canadian national health program have overhead costs of only 2 to 3 percent. The complexity of our current insurance system, with its multiplicity of payers, forces U.S. hospitals to spend more than twice as much as Canadian hospitals on billing and administration and requires U.S. physicians to spend about 10 percent of their gross incomes on excess billing costs.[1] Eliminating insurance programs that duplicated the national health program coverage, though politically thorny, would clearly be within the prerogative of Congress.[2] Failure to do so would also require the continuation of the costly bureaucracy necessary to administer and deal with such programs.

Copayments and deductibles endanger the health of poor people who are sick,[3] decrease the use of vital inpatient medical services as much as they discourage the use of unnecessary ones,[4] discourage preventive care,[5] and are unwieldy and expensive to administer. Canada has few such charges, yet health costs are lower than in the United States and have risen slowly.[6,7] In the United States , in contrast, increasing co-payments and deductibles have failed to slow the escalation of costs.

Instead of the confused and often unjust dictates of insurance companies, a greatly expanded program of technology assessment and cost-effectiveness evaluation would guide decisions about covered services, as well as about the allocation of funds for capital spending, drug formulas, and other issues.

Payment for Hospital Services

Each hospital would receive a lump-sum payment to cover all operating expenses—a "global" budget. The amount of this payment would be negotiated with the state national health program payment board and would be based on past expenditures, previous financial and clinical performance, projected changes in levels of services, wages and other costs, and proposed new and innovative programs. Hospitals would not bill for service covered by the national health program. No part of the operating budget could be used for hospital expansion, profit, marketing, or major capital purchases or leases. These expenditures would also come from the national health program fund, but monies for them would be appropriated separately.

Global prospective budgeting would simplify hospital administration and virtually eliminate billing, thus freeing up substantial resources for increased clinical care. Before the nationwide implementation of the national program, hospitals in the states with demonstration programs could bill out-of-state patients on a simple per diem basis. Prohibiting the use of operating funds for capital purchases or profit would eliminate the main financial incentive for both excessive intervention (under fee-for-service payment) and skimping on care (under DRG-type prospective payment systems), since neither inflating revenues nor limiting care would result in gain for the institution. The separate appropriation of funds explicitly designated for capital expenditures would facilitate rational health planning. In Canada, this method of hospital payment has been successful in containing costs, minimizing bureaucracy, improving

273

the distribution of health resources, and maintaining the quality of care.[6-9] It shifts the focus of hospital administration away from the bottom line and toward the provision of optimal clinical services.

Payment for Physician Services, Ambulatory Care, and Medical Home Care

To minimize the disruption of existing patterns of care, the national health program would include three payment options for physicians and other practitioners: fee-for-service payment, salaried positions in institutions receiving global budgets, and salaried positions within group practices or HMOs receiving per capita (capitation) payments.

Fee-for-Service Payment

The state national health program payment board and a representative of the fee-for-service practitioners (perhaps the state medical society) would negotiate a simplified, binding fee schedule. Physicians would submit bills to the national health program on a simple form or by computer and would receive extra payment for any bill not paid within 30 days. Payments to physician would cover only the service provided by physicians and their support staff and would exclude reimbursement for costly capital purchases of equipment for the office, such as CT scanners. Physicians who accepted payment from the national health program could bill patients directly only for uncovered services (as is done for cosmetic surgery in Canada).

Global Budgets

Institutions such as hospitals, health centers, group practices, clinics serving migrant workers, and medical home care agencies could elect to receive a global budget for the delivery of outpatient home care, and physicians' services, as well as for preventive health care and patient-education programs. The negotiation process and the regulations covering capital expenditures and profits would be similar to those for inpatient hospital services. Physicians employed in such institutions would be salaried.

Capitation

HMOs, group practices, and other institutions could elect to be paid fees on a per capita basis to cover all outpatient care, physicians' services, and medical home care. The regulations covering the use of such payments for capital expenditures and for profits would be similar to those that would apply to hospitals. The capitation fee would not cover inpatient services (except care provided by a physician), which would be included in hospitals' global budgets. Selective enrollment policies would be prohibited, and patients would be permitted to leave an HMO or other health plan with appropriate notice. Physicians working in HMOs would be salaried, and financial incentives to physicians based on the HMO's financial performance would be prohibited.

The diversity of existing practice arrangements, each with strong proponents, necessitates a pluralistic approach. Under all three proposed options, capital purchase and profits would be uncoupled from payments to physicians and other operating costs—a feature that is essential for minimizing entrepreneurial incentives, containing costs, and facilitating health planning.

Under the fee-for-service option, physicians' office overhead would be reduced by the simplification of billing.[1] The improved coverage would encourage preventive care.[10] In Canada, fee-for-service practice with negotiated fee schedules and mandatory assignment (acceptance of the assigned fee as total payment) has proved to be compatible with cost containment, adequate incomes for physicians, and a high level of access to and satisfaction with care on the part of patients.[6,7] The Canadian provinces have responded to the inflationary potential of fee-for-service payment in various ways: by limiting the number of physicians, by monitoring physicians for outlandish practice patterns, by setting overall limits on a province's spending for physicians' services (thus relying on the profession to police itself), and even by capping the total reimbursement of individual physicians. These regulatory options have been made possible (and have not required an extensive bureaucracy) because all payment comes from a single source. Similar measures might be needed in the United States, although our penchant for bureaucratic hypertrophy might require a concomitant cap on spending for the regulatory apparatus. For example, spending for program administration and reimbursement bureaucracy might be restricted to 3 percent of total costs.

Global budgets for institutional providers would eliminate billing, while providing a predictable and stable source of income. Such funding could also encourage the development of preventive health programs in the community, such as education programs on the acquired immunodeficiency syndrome (AIDS), whose costs are difficult to attribute and bill to individual patients.

Continuity of care would no longer be disrupted when patients' insurance coverage changed as a result of retirement or a job change. Incentives for providers receiving capitation payments to skimp on care would be minimized, since unused operating funds could not be devoted to expansion or profit.

Payment for Long-Term Care

A separate proposal for long-term care is under development, guided by three principles. First, access to care should be based on need rather than on age or ability to pay. Second, social and community-based services should be expanded and integrated with institutional care. Third, bureaucracy and entrepreneurial incentives should be minimized through global budgeting with separate funding for capital expenses.

Allocation of Capital Funds, Health Planning, and Return on Equity

Funds for the construction or renovation of health facilities and for purchases of major equipment would be appropriated from the national health program budget. The funds would be distributed by state and regional health-planning boards composed of both experts and representatives. Capital projects funded by private donations would require approval by the health-planning board if they entailed an increase in future operating expenses.

The national health program would pay owners of for-profit hospitals, nursing homes, and clinics a reasonable fixed rate of return on existing equity. Since virtually all new capital investment would be funded by the national health program, it would not be included in calculating the return on equity.

Current capital spending greatly affects future operating cost, as well as the distribution of resources. Effective health planning requires that funds go to high-quality, efficient programs in the areas of greatest need. Under the existing reimbursement system, which combines operating and capital payments, prosperous hospitals can expand and modernize, whereas impoverished ones cannot, regardless of the health needs of the population they serve or the quality of service they provide. The national health program would replace this implicit mechanism for distributing capital with an explicit one, which would facilitate (though not guarantee) allocation on the basis of need and equality. Insulating these crucial decisions from distortion by narrow interests would require the rigorous evaluation of the technology and assessment of needs, as well as the active involvement of providers and patients.

For-profit providers would be compensated for existing investments. Since new for-profit investment would be barred, the proprietary sector would gradually shrink.

Public, Environmental, and Occupational Health Services

Existing arrangements for public, occupational, and environmental health services would be retained in the short term. Funding for preventive health care would be expanded. Additional proposals dealing with these issues are planned.

Prescription Drugs and Supplies

An expert panel would establish and regularly update a list of all necessary and useful drugs and outpatient equipment. Suppliers would bill the national health program directly for the wholesale cost, plus a reasonable dispensing fee, of any item in the list that was prescribed by a licensed practitioner. The substitution of generic for proprietary drugs would be encouraged.

Funding

The national health program would disburse virtually all payments for health service. The total expenditure would be set at the same proportion of the GNP as health costs represented in the year preceding the establishment of the national health program. Funds for the national health program could be raised through a variety of mechanisms. In the long run, funding based on an income tax or other progressive tax might be the fairest and most efficient solution, since tax-based funding is the least cumbersome and least expensive mechanism for collecting money. During the transition period in states with demonstration programs, the following structure would mimic existing funding patterns and minimize economic disruption.

Medicare and Medicaid

All current and federal funds allocated to Medicare and Medicaid would be paid to the national health program. The contribution of each program would be based on the previous year's expenditures, adjusted for inflation. Using Medicare and Medicaid funds in this manner would require a federal waiver.

State and Local Funds

All current state and local funds for health care expenditures, adjusted for inflation, would be paid to the national health program.

Employer Contributions

A tax earmarked for the national health program would be levied on all employers. The tax rate would be set so that total collections equaled the previous year's statewide total of employers' expenditures for health benefits, adjusted for inflation. Employers obligated by pre-existing contracts to provide health benefits could credit the cost of those benefits toward their national health program tax liability.

Private Insurance Revenues

Private health insurance plans duplicating the coverage of the national health program would be phased out over three years. During this transition period, all revenues from such plans would be turned over to the national health program, after the deduction of a reasonable fee to cover the costs of collecting premiums.

General Tax Revenues

Additional taxes, equivalent to the amount now spent by individual citizens for insurance premiums and out-of-pocket health costs, would be levied.

It would be critical for all funds for health care to flow through the national health program. Such single-source payment (monopsony) has been the cornerstone of cost containment and health planning in Canada. The mechanism of raising funds for the national health program would be a matter of tax policy, largely separate from the organization of the health care system itself. As in Canada, federal funding could attenuate inequalities among the states in financial and medical resources.

The transitional proposal for demonstration programs in selected states illustrates how monopsony payment could be established with limited disruption of existing patterns of health care funding. The employers' contribution would represent a decrease in costs for most firms that now provide health insurance and an increase for those that do not currently pay for benefits. Some provision might be needed to cushion the impact of the change on financially strapped small businesses. Decreased individual spending for health care would offset the additional tax burden on individual citizens.

Private health insurance, with its attendant inefficiency and waste, would be largely eliminated. A program of job replacement and retraining for insurance and hospital-billing employees would be an important component of the program during the transition period.

Discussion

The Patient's View

The national health program would establish a right to comprehensive health care. As in Canada, each person would receive a national health program card entitling him or her to all necessary medical care without co-payments or deductibles. The card could be used with any fee-for-service practitioner and at any institution receiving a global budget. HMO members could receive non-emergency care only through their HMO, although they could readily transfer to the non-HMO option.

Thus, patients would have a free choice of providers, and the financial threat of illness would be eliminated. Taxes would increase by an amount equivalent to the current total of medical expenditures by individuals. Conversely, individuals' aggregate payments for medical care would decrease by the same amount.

The Practitioner's View

Physicians would have a free choice of practice settings. Treatment would no longer be constrained by the patient's insurance status or by bureaucratic dicta. On the basis of the Canadian experience, we anticipate that the average physician's income would change little, although differences among specialties might be attenuated.

Fee-for-service practitioners would be paid for the care of anyone not enrolled in an HMO. The entrepreneurial aspects of medicine—with the attendant problems as well as possibilities—would be limited. Physicians could concentrate on medicine; every patient would be fully insured, but physicians could increase their income only by providing more care. Billing would involve imprinting the patient's national health program card on a charge slip, checking a box to indicate the complexity of the procedure or service, and sending the slip (or computer record) to the physician-payment board. This simplification of billing would save thousands of dollars per practitioner in annual office expenses.[1]

Bureaucratic interference in clinical decision making would sharply diminish. Costs would be contained by controlling overall spending and by limiting entrepreneurial incentives, thus obviating the need for the kind of detailed administrative oversight that is characteristic of the DRG program and similar schemes. Indeed, there is much less administrative intrusion in day-to-day clinical practice in Canada (and most other countries with national health programs) than in the United States. [11,12]

Salaried practitioners would be insulated from the financial consequences of clinical decisions. Because savings on patient care could no longer be used for institutional expansion or profits, the pressure to skimp on care would be minimized.

The Effect on Other Health Workers

Nurses and other health care personnel would enjoy a more humane and efficient clinical milieu. The burdens of paperwork associated with billing would be lightened. The jobs of many administrative and insurance employees would be eliminated, necessitating a major effort at job placement and retraining. We advocate that any of these displaced workers be deployed in expanded programs of public health, health promotion and education, and home care and as support personnel to free nurses for clinical tasks.

The Effect on Hospitals

Hospitals' revenues would become stable and predictable. More than half the current hospital bureaucracy would be eliminated,[1] and the remaining administrators could focus on facilitating clinical care and planning for future health needs.

The capital budget requests of hospitals would be weighed against other priorities for health care investment. Hospitals would neither grow because they were profitable nor fail because of unpaid bills—although regional health planning would undoubtedly mandate that some expand and others close or be put to other uses. Responsiveness to community needs, the quality of care, efficiency, and innovation would replace financial performance as the bottom line. The elimination of new for-profit investment would lead to a gradual conversion of proprietary hospitals to not-for-profit status.

The Effect on the Insurance Industry

The insurance industry would feel the greatest impact of this proposal. Private insurance firms would have no role in health care financing, since the public administration of insurance is more efficient,[1,13] and single-source payment is the key to both equal access and cost control. Indeed, most of the extra funds needed to finance the expansion of care would come from eliminating the overhead and profits of insurance companies and abolishing the billing apparatus necessary to apportion costs among the various plans.

The Effect on Corporate America

Firms that now provide generous employee health benefits would realize savings, because their contribution to the national health program would be less than their current health insurance costs. For example, health care expenditures by Chrysler, currently $5,300 annually per employee,[14] would fall to about $1,600, a figure calculated by dividing the total current U.S. spending on health by private employers by the total number of full-time-equivalent, non-government employees. Since most firms that compete in international markets would save money, the competitiveness of U.S. products would be enhanced. However, costs would increase for employers that do not now provide health benefits. The average health care costs for employers would be unchanged in the short run. In the long run, overall health costs would rise less steeply because of improved health planning and greater efficiency. The funding mechanism ultimately adopted would determine the corporate share of those costs.

Health Benefits and Financial Costs

There is ample evidence that removing financial barriers to health care encourages timely care and improves health. After Canada instituted a national health program, visits to physicians increased among patients with serious symptoms.[15] Mortality rates, which were higher than U.S. rates through the 1950s and early 1960s, fell below those in the United States.[1] In the Rand Health Insurance Experiment, free care reduced the annual risk of dying by 10 percent among the 25 percent of U.S. adults at highest risk.[3] Conversely, cuts in California's Medicaid program led to worsening health.[17] Strong circumstantial evidence links the poor U.S. record on infant mortality with inadequate access to prenatal care.[18]

We expect that the national health program would cause little change in the total costs of ambulatory and hospital care; savings on administration and billing (about 10 percent of current health care spending[1]) would approximately offset the costs of expanded services.[19,20] Indeed, current low hospital-occupancy rates suggest that the additional care could be provided at low cost. Similarly, many physicians with empty appointment slots could take on more patients without added office, secretarial, or other overhead costs. However, the expansion of long-term care (under any system) would increase costs. The experience in Canada suggests that the increased demand for acute care would be modest after an initial surge,[21,22] and that improvements in health planning[8] and cost containment made possible by single source payment[9] would slow the escalation of health care costs. Vigilance would be needed to stem the regrowth of costly and intrusive bureaucracy.

Unsolved Problems

Our brief proposal leaves many vexing problems unsolved. Much detailed planning would be needed to ease dislocations during the implementation of the program. Neither the encouragement of preventive health care and healthful life styles nor improvements in occupational and environmental health would automatically follow from the institution of a national health program. Similarly, racial, linguistic, geographic, and other nonfinancial barriers to access would persist. The need for quality assurance and continuing medical education would be no less pressing. High medical school tuitions that skew specialty choices and discourage low-income applicants, the underrepresentation of minorities, the role of foreign medical graduates, and other issues in medical education would remain. Some patients would still seek inappropriate emergency care, and some physicians might still succumb to the temptation to increase their incomes by encouraging unneeded services. The malpractice crisis would be only partially ameliorated. The 25 percent of judgments now awarded for future medical costs would be eliminated but our society would remain litigious, and legal and insurance fees would still consume about two-thirds of all malpractice premiums.[23] Establishing research priorities and directing funds to high-quality investigations would be no easier. Much further work in the area of long-term care would be required. Regional health planning and capital allocation would make possible, but not ensure, the fair and efficient allocation of resources. Finally, although insurance coverage for patients with AIDS would be ensured, the need for expanded prevention and research and for new models of care would continue. Although all these problems would not be solved, a national health program would establish a framework for addressing them.

Political Prospects

Our proposal would undoubtedly encounter powerful opponents in the health insurance industry, firms that do not provide health benefits to employees, and medical entrepreneurs. However, we also have allies. Most physicians (56 percent) support some form of national health program, although 74 percent are convinced that most other doctors oppose it.[24] Many of the largest corporations would enjoy substantial savings if our proposal were adopted. Most significant, the great majority of Americans support a universal, comprehensive, publicly administered national health program, as shown virtually by virtually every opinion poll in the past 30 years.[25,26] Indeed, a 1986 referendum question in Massachusetts calling for a national health program was approved two to one, carrying all 39 cities and 307 of the 312 towns in the commonwealth.[27] If mobilized, such public conviction could override even the most strenuous private opposition.

References

1. Himmelstein DU, Woolhandler S. Cost without benefit: administrative waste in U.S. health care. N Engl J Med 1986; 314:441-5.

2. Advisory opinion regarding House of Representatives Bill 85-H-7748 (No. 86-269-MP, R.I. Sup. Ct. Jan 5, 1987).

3. Brook RH, Ware JE Jr, Rogers WH, et al. Does free care improve adults' health? Results from a randomized controlled trial. N Engl J Med 1983; 309:1426-34.

4. Siu AL, Sonnenberg FA, Manning WG, et al. Inappropriate use of hospitals in a randomized trial of health insurance plans. N Engl J Med 1986; 315:1259-66.

5. Brian EW, Gibbens SF. California's Medi-Cal copayment experiment. Med Care 1974; 12:Suppl 12:1-303.

6. Iglehart JK. Canada's health care system. N Engl of Med 1986; 315:202-8, 778-84.

7. Idem. Canada's health care system: addressing the problem of physician supply. N Engl J Med 1986; 315:1623-8.

8. Detsky AS, Stacey SR, Bombardier C. The effectiveness of a regulatory strategy in containing hospital costs: the Ontario experience, 1967-1981. N Engl J Med 1983; 309:151-9.

9. Evans RG. Health care in Canada: patterns of funding and regulation. In: McLachlan G, Maynard A, eds. The public/private mix for health: the relevance and effects of change. London: Nuffield Provincial Hospitals Trust, 1982:369-424.

10. Woolhandler S, Himmelstein DU. Reverse targeting of preventive care due to lack of health insurance. JAMA 1988; 259:2872-4.

11. Reinhardt UE. Resource allocation in health care: the allocation of lifestyles to providers. Milbank Q 1987; 65:153-76.

12. Hoffenberg R. Clinical freedom. London: Nuffield Provincial Hospitals Trust, 1987.

13. Horn JM, Beck RG. Further evidence on public versus private administration of health insurance. J Public Health Policy 1981; 2:274-90.

14. Cronin C. Next Congress to grapple with U.S. health policy, competitiveness abroad. Bus Health 1986; 4(2):55.

15. Enterline PE, Salter V, McDonald AD, McDonald JC. The distribution of medical services before and after "free" medical care—the Quebec experience. N Engl J Med 1973;289:1174-8.

16. Roemer R, Roemer MI. Health manpower policy under national health insurance: the Canadian experience. Hyattsville, Md.: Health Resources Administration, 1977. (DHEW publication no. (HRA) 77-37.)

17. Lurie N, Ward NB, Shapiro MF, et al. Termination of Medi-Cal benefits: a followup study one year later. N Engl J Med 1986; 314:1266-8.

18. Institute of Medicine. Preventing low birthweight. Washington, D.C.:

287

THE NATIONAL HEALTH PROGRAM BOOK

National Academy Press, 1985.

19. Newhouse JP, Manning WG, Morris CN, et al. Some interim results from a controlled trial of cost sharing in health insurance. N Engl J Med 1981; 305:1501-7.

20. Himmelstein DU, Woolhandler S. Free care: a quantitative analysis of the health and cost effects of a national program. In J Health Serv 1988; 18:393-9.

21. LeClair M. The Canadian health care system. In: Andreopoulos S, ed. National health insurance: can we learn from Canada? New York: John Wiley, 1975:11-92.

22. Evans RG. Beyond the medical marketplace: expenditure, utilization and pricing of insured health care in Canada. In: Andreopoulos S, ed. National health insurance: can we learn from Canada? New York: John Wiley, 1975:129-78.

23. Danzon PM. Medical malpractice: theory, evidence, and public policy. Cambridge, Mass.: Harvard University Press, 1985.

24. Colombotas J, Kirchner C. Physicians and social change. New York: Oxford University Press, 1985.

25. Navarro V. Where is the popular mandate? N Engl J Med 1982; 307:1516-8.

26. Pokorny G. Report card on health care. Health Manage Q 1988; 10(1):3-7.

27. Danielson DA, Mazer A. Results of the Massachusetts Referendum on a national health program. J Public Health Policy 1987; 8:28-35.